MARION COTILLARD

Dominique Choulant

MARION COTILLARD
Biography

Éditions L'Entretemps/Max Milo

ISBN : 978-2-31501-144-5

"On a trip to India, I met someone who said to me, "Accept your desire, accept your ambition, accept that you are someone who can crave seduction, because until you accept that, you can't get past it." That phrase, I take with me."

Marion Cotillard, *Gala*, n° 535,
September 10, 2003.

"I hope that when I'm 40, I won't need the other person's gaze anymore. Old actresses are pathetic. The need for seduction is a young person's thing, right?"

Marion Cotillard, *Libération*,
February 9, 2006.

Acknowledgements

Chantal Delmont / INA Pyrénées, for her kindness and for giving her access to the television archives;

the staff of the library of the Toulouse Cinematheque, for their helpfulness;

Sophie Bourahla / City Hall of Paris 12th district, for her assistance;

François Bagnaud & Gérard Blua, for their constant friendly support throughout this work.

Childhood, Entering the scene

The year 1975 is decreed by the UN[1] "International Women's Year". Yes, as Jean Ferrat sings so well, *Woman is the future of man*, a title borrowed from the famous maxim of Aragon. But, after *Le Zizi* "en or massif" by Pierre Perret, it is Alain Barrière, in duet with Noëlle Cordier, who gets the (unexpected) jackpot of the year with the romantic slow song *Tu t'en vas*. Let's not forget *L'Été indien*, a summer hit immortalized by Joe Dassin, or *Le Sud*, number 1 in all the charts, which marks the return of Nino Ferrer with this melancholic, timeless ritornello...

"It's a place that feels like Louisiana,
To Italy
There is laundry on the terrace
And it's pretty
It looks like the South
The time lasts a long time,
And life surely
More than a million years
And always in summer [...]."

1. The United Nations.

In the cinema, we can cite some major films released that year: *The Towering Inferno* with Paul Newman, Steve McQueen, William Holden and Faye Dunaway; *Fear in the City* with Jean-Paul Belmondo; *We found the 7th Company!* with Jean Lefebvre, Pierre Mondy and Henri Guybet; *Histoire d'O* by Just Jaeckin and *The Old Gun* with Philippe Noiret and Romy Schneider mark the top of the French *box office*.

In February 1975, Annie Girardot was elected "favorite female star of 1974" by the readers of *Ciné-Revue*, ahead of Romy Schneider, Mireille Darc, Sophia Loren and Catherine Deneuve, while among male actors, Alain Delon dominated against Jean Gabin, Charles Bronson, Paul Newman and Jean-Paul Belmondo.

At the international level, Isabelle Adjani, at just 20 years old, makes a name for herself with *L'Histoire d'Adèle H.* by François Truffaut and her name is on everyone's lips. It is also the year when great actors of French cinema leave us: Pierre Fresnay, the *Marius* of Marcel Pagnol; Michel Simon, the *Boudu sauvé des eaux* of Jean Renoir; Josephine Baker, *The Siren of the Tropics* of the 1920s and the young Pierre Blaise, the *Lacombe Lucien* of Louis Malle.

And, in the midst of all these events, on September 30, 1975 - while in several cities in America we celebrate the twenty-fifth anniversary of the death of James Dean[2] - in Paris, in the 12th arrondissement, at 4:50 am, Monique Theillaud[3], 23, gave birth to a daughter. With her companion Jean-Claude Cotillard, 29 years old, she decided to call her Marion.

"Four years after Marion, our sons were born, twins[4]", as Jean-Claude Cotillard explains.

Their names are Guillaume and Quentin.

Monique Theillaud and Jean-Claude Cotillard met in the amateur theater network. She is an actress. He, mime in his spare time[5] and teaches body expression.

During the years that follow, the five Cotillards form a little troupe unlike any other, who, aboard a van that serves as a hotel, will carry their dreams and their little talents around without seeing the darkness of the world. The parents have founded a traveling theater for children and offer tales in which Marion, Guillaume and Quentin are the heroes.

---

2. James DEAN (1931-1955), American actor, hero of *East of Eden, Fury of Life* and *Giant*.
3. Since then, Monique has been renamed "Niseema" by a master in spiritual research.
4. "Marion Cotillard, le sacre", *Paris Match*, n° 3067 28 February 2008.
5. He was trained at the school of Maximilien Decroux.

At that time, the Cotillards lived in Alfortville, in the southern suburbs of Paris, at the top of a tower block in the middle of a housing estate that Marion found marvelous: "There was the whole world in my building[6]. And also dope and hooligans, which make life difficult. Then when the eldest was ten years old, the Cotillard family left to live in the countryside of Orleans. There, everyone is white, except Marion's only friend, who is Moroccan. "One day, some guys from school trapped me under a staircase and sprayed me with cologne to clean me up. I learned what racism was[7]." Between the ages of 10 and 15, she doesn't remember much other than a difference that is heavy to bear:

> "I felt vapid and characterless. I wanted to be anyone but myself, anywhere but where I belonged. I wanted to disappear, lest I be called a skull[8]."

A loner at heart, Marion Cotillard lived "an autistic adolescence", according to her own words[9].

Everything will be better in 1990, when she leaves the Victor Hugo college in Puiseaux and enters the

6. Pascale NivElle, "Portrait Édith donc...", *Libération*, February 9, 2006.
7. *Ibid.*
8. *Ibid.*
9. *Ciné-Télé-Revue*, n° 39, September 26, 2002.

Voltaire high school in Orleans, where she chooses a theater option. Marion Cotillard then found her vocation and enrolled at the Orleans Conservatory a year later. If her father works there, she does not get any special treatment.

"When Marion told me she wanted to enter the Conservatory, I told her she just had to take the entrance exam [10]", says Jean-Claude Cotillard, who was in charge of the drama department at the time. Marion then became the youngest person admitted to the conservatory and one of its best elements.

> The little Cotillard was extremely talented," recalls Nicole Mérouze, her drama teacher. She was very pretty but she also had a presence, a personality. She stood out from the crowd. She was ambitious in her choices. In my class, she had chosen to work on the role of the little queen in Shakespeare's *Richard III*. A difficult character, at the height of her passions.

The alumna's career doesn't surprise the now-retired teacher:

> "I was sure she would do this job. It was in every pore of her skin. It's not a flame in her eyes, but a home [11]."

10. lepoint.fr, March 27, 2008.
11. lepoint.fr, March 27, 2008.

With her baccalaureate in her pocket at the age of 18, Marion immediately got down to business. In other words, the concrete, the castings. She was taken very quickly, carrying like a medal not only the First Prize of the Conservatory of Dramatic Art of Orleans obtained in June 1994 but above all, a sentence bequeathed by her beloved mother: "In life, everything is a gift. The problem is that sometimes it is badly wrapped[12].

Monique and Jean-Claude's only concern in raising their children was to teach them freedom, curiosity and a distrust of convention and formatting. The only parental requirements were to speak English perfectly, to know how to drive and to never let anyone decide for them. "If you are free, devoid of material greed and with an ordinary ego, it is easier to go where you want to go," according to Jean-Claude Cotillard[13], now a recognized director[14] and director of ESAD[15] since 2003 and until 2013.

12. Pascale Niv*Elle*, "Portrait Édith donc...", *Libération*, February 9, 2006.
13. "Marion Cotillard, le rêve américain", *Paris Match*, n° 3170, February 18, 2010.
14. He won the Molière 2006 for best private theater show for Moi aussi, je suis Catherine Deneuve by Pierre Notte and the Molière 2010 for best musical show for Les Douze Pianos d'Hercule by Jean-Paul Farré.
15. École supérieure d'art dramatique de la ville de Paris.

But, as we know, there is no actor without an ego.

The ego is like cholesterol," continues Jean-Claude Cotillard, "there are good and bad! There must be a balance. For the actor, the balance must be between humility and insolence. Without humility, there is no creativity. But without insolence, where to find the incredible courage to enter the scene?

Marion Cotillard makes her first appearance in the cinema in *L'Histoire du garçon qui voulait qu'on l'embrasse*. This film, released on March 23, 1994, is the second feature film by Philippe Harel, who shows us the ordinary life of a young solitary student (played by Julien Collet) in search of his first kiss. Unfortunately, this little-known production only attracts a confidential audience since it does not count more than 23,552 entries.

"With his first film, which he also starred in, *Un été sans histoire* (medium-length film), Philippe Harel found an original tone. A falsely disillusioned nonchalance, an acidic humor and a corrosive spontaneity that suggested a real potential. Unfortunately, these qualities are not found in The *Boy Who Wanted to be Kissed*. It must be said that the script, obviously autobiographical, written several years ago, should have been his first film if he had found a producer. He is now shooting it, but it lacks a radical energy. Philippe Harel is no longer the teenager he was and the generation he films is no longer his own. This gap diminishes the strength of his vision and gives his film a somewhat sterile languor. This does not take anything away from his talent. We simply have the feeling that he wears this film a bit like a garment that no longer fits. We are already waiting for the next[16]."

No matter: Marion Cotillard has taken the cinema by storm! We can say that everything is going very fast and easy for the beautiful French woman:

"I had a pretty immediate relationship with the camera, I was never afraid[17]."

16. It will be Les Randonneurs in 1997, with Karin Viard, Geraldine Pailhas Benoît Poelvoorde, Vincent Elbaz and Philippe Harel himself. Christophe D'YVOIRE, *Studio Magazine*, n° 85, April 1994.
17. Interview by Thierry Chèze in *Studio Magazine*, n° 173, December 2001, p. 130-131.

ON THE ROAD TO FAME

To be more precise, Marion Cotillard got her first role for television in 1982 in the short film *Le Monde des tout-petits* by Claude Cailloux. The following year, she turns again for this director in *Lucie*. She also appeared in the video clip *Petite fille des Wampas* - featured on the album *Les Wampas... vous aiment,* released in April 1990 - and then in one of the ads against alcoholism in the first series, signed by Gérard Jugnot, of *Tu t'es vu quand t'as bu?* - *a* slogan that marked several generations - as well as in two episodes of the first season of the television series *Highlander* in 1992 and 1993. But it is thanks to the hectic *Taxi* by Gérard Pirès, produced by Luc Besson, that Marion Cotillard is revealed to the general public in April 1998. 6.5 million spectators came to follow the adventures of Daniel, a cab driver from Marseille with a big heart and world champion of driving at full speed, who is brought against his will to team up with a clumsy and unlucky policeman whom he will take in friendship. Daniel is, as everyone knows, played by Samy Naceri and the inspector by Frédéric Diefenthal.

Marion Cotillard, the fiancée of the driving mad hero, is then 22 years old: from then on her career undergoes a nice boost.

Between Philippe Harel's film and that of Gérard Pirès, let's not forget that her career is marked by the series *Extreme Limit* in 1994, a few short films and several TV movies - including *Chloe* in 1996. That year, she also appeared twice in the cinema: in *Comment je me suis disputé... (ma vie sexuelle)*, a film by Arnaud Desplechin, remarkable for some, detestable for others, and in *La Belle Verte*, a failed shot by Coline Serreau.

The following year, she got a role in *The Seagull, one of* the ten short films that make up *Love is to be Reinvented*, a film about homosexuality and bisexuality in the time of AIDS.

The young actress also appeared on the stage of the Théâtre contemporain de la danse in Paris for *Y'a des nounours dans les placards*, a choreographic piece directed in 1997 by her cousin Laurent Cotillard.

But, as mentioned above, it was in 1998, when the film *Taxi was* released in theaters, that her career took a real turn. That same year, the actress made her first steps on the red carpet in Cannes and the following year obtained a first nomination for the César.

"I would never have imagined the magnitude of the phenomenon[18], and even less to be included in it having shot only ten days[19]!"

If Marion Cotillard's career was previously based on rare and very intimate works, this film has undeniably changed her life as an actress since she had considered, at a very young age, giving up everything:

"When I shot it, I hadn't worked in two years[20]."

Marion completes her remarks:

"In the midst of my post-adolescence years, I felt bad about myself and was totally lost when faced with this profession, which I didn't understand any of the rules[21]."

But the *Taxi* storm sweeps away everything in its path, including Marion's modesty.

"The first public screenings were very violent. I was not prepared for this media coverage, but Luc Besson protected me enormously[22]."

18. The filming of the movie took place in Marseille in 27 days: from August 4 to 31, 1997.
19. Interview by Thierry Chèze in *Studio Magazine*, n° 173, December 2001.
20. *Télé-Poche*, n° 1787, May 8, 2000.
21. Interview by Thierry Chèze in *Studio Magazine*, n° 173, December 2001, p. 130-131.
22. *Ibid.*

However, our deer in the rough would have committed a blunder towards Luc Besson during the casting of *Taxi*.

> "There were many candidates. As I had been told that I had to break through before 25 years old, or else I was screwed, I put a lot of pressure on myself, like "it's Besson or knitting". When I arrived in front of Luc, I explained to him that I preferred small intimate films. He had just finished *The Fifth Element*. I thought I would never get the part, but strangely enough, two weeks later, I got a call to offer it to him[23].

"When the casting director told me the good news, I thought it was a joke[24] !

This film brings her a new recognition from the profession, but also from the street. A phenomenon that she manages with difficulty.

> "I was uncomfortable with people coming up to me. I was unable to respond to them and would often break down in tears. I had to put up barriers[25]."

On March 6, 1999, under the leadership of the president Isabelle Huppert, we discover the winner

---

23. *Ciné-Télé-Revue*, n° 39, September 26, 2002.
24. *Télé 7 jours*, n°. 2721, July 21, 2012.
25. Interview by Thierry Chèze in *Studio Magazine*, n° 173, December 2001, p. 130-131.

of the best female hope of the 24th ceremony of the César. If it is not Marion Cotillard but (unsurprisingly) Natacha Régnier for *La Vie rêvée des anges* by Érick Zonca[26], our actress - as Samy Naceri's girlfriend whose ardor is always thwarted - has nevertheless succeeded with vivacity and determination in imposing her character against the devastating male "couple". No one can therefore dispute the improvement.

In May 1999, she made her second ascent of the steps in Cannes, for the 52nd edition of the most mediatized festival in the world (that year, the Palme d'Or went to the Dardenne brothers for *Rosetta*).

On his way to fame, we find his charming little face in two films: *The War in the High Country* and *From Blue to America*.

The first, based on the novel of the same name by Charles-Ferdinand Ramuz, was released on April 21, 1999.

> "Co-written by Jean-Claude Carrière, the eighth film by Swiss director Francis Reusser *(Derborence)* is a story of thwarted love in the Pays de Vaud at the end of the 18th century, in the middle of the Napoleonic conquest. It is, unfortunately, served by a too classical tone and an overly

----

26. Nominated seven times, *Taxi* won the César for best sound (Vincent Tulli and Vincent Arnardi) and best editing (Véronique Lange).

theatrical staging, to which only the actors (Yann Trégouët, François Marthouret and Marion Cotillard, touching romantic heroine) manage to give a little air[27].

The second one is presented to us on December 1st, 1999.

The story: victim of a serious accident, Camille (Samuel Jouy) is admitted in a rehabilitation center. He falls in love with Solange (Marion Cotillard), paralyzed like him.

Looking at its synopsis, this first feature film by Sarah Lévy - inspired by her own experience - could be off-putting. Wrongly so. "More than a film about disability, *From Blue to America* is above all a love story. The real one, the one that can move mountains... or open the path to recovery. The one that unites Camille and Solange, brilliantly played by Samuel Jouy and Marion Cotillard. A film in their image: both radiant and feverish[28].

However, both were abysmal failures: *La Guerre dans le Haut Pays (War in the High Country)* had 1,544 entries in France and *Du bleu jusqu'en Amérique (Blue to America)* had 1,226.

----

27. Thierry Chèze's comments in *Studio Magazine*, n° 144, April 1999.
28. Thierry Chèze's comments in *Studio Magazine*, n° 151, December 1999.

It is then a real disappointment for actors in general and for Marion Cotillard[29] in particular. The young actress wanted, with these roles, to prove herself with radical and independent choices, far from her character in *Taxi*, which helped to make her known. However, the major success met by the first part, will lead her to find the panoply of Lilly Bertineau for a new opus.

While waiting for the continuation of the adventures of Daniel and Émilien, his career takes shape at the mythical Studio Harcourt, created in 1934, which is an essential place for any actor in search of posterity.

This year 1999, Marion Cotillard is photographed there: "In France, one is not an actor if one has not been photographed by the Harcourt Studio[30]", wrote the great writer Roland Barthes in 1957.

Curiously, it seems that Marion Cotillard does not like herself much on the photograph that symbolizes her entry into the legend. However, her pretty face, her original pose and her look towards

29. Which was nonetheless rewarded, in December 1999, at the 16th Autrans Mountain Film Festival (Rhône-Alpes), with a special mention for the film La Guerre dans le Haut Pays.
30. Dominique BAQUÉ and Françoise DENOY*Elle*, Studio Harcourt, cinquante ans de mythes étoilés, La Manufacture, Lyon, 1991.

the future are those of an actress at the dawn of a superb career.

So, with the support of a luxurious black and white photograph, she is still allowed to dream. But what does our actress really dream of in the year 2000? "I dream of a day when all the beings of this planet would live, only one minute, at the same moment, "the present moment"... just to see[31]..."

At the time of this revelation, on March 29, 2000, *Taxi 2 was* released, an almost inevitable sequel featuring the same duo of actors, but this time with Gérard Krawczyk as director, Gérard Pirès not being confirmed as director. Although everyone expects another big success, it is in fact a real tidal wave: the film has the best first day and first week of all time in France! The film, which started off with a bang at the box office, achieved the highest number of admissions in France for the year 2000 (with 10 million spectators). This success confirms the intuition of Luc Besson, producer and scriptwriter of the film, and the popularity of Samy Naceri and Frédéric Diefenthal with the public. The public welcomes them like *rock stars as* soon as they appear on the screen and gives them a triumph every time they appear in broad daylight,

---

31. "À quoi rêvent les actrices ?", *Studio Magazine*, n° 154, March 2000, p. 113.

as is the case in May at the Cannes Film Festival[32]. As for the girls of *Taxi 2*, Marion Cotillard - the brunette - and Emma Sjöberg - the blonde - are not to be outdone: "We could not imagine such a success", they say on the front page of the weekly magazine *Télé-Poche* No. 1787, of May 8. One question is obvious for Marion Cotillard: does her sudden notoriety bother her? "It has not changed my life. Simply, when I walk in the street, I am recognized more and more often. But people rarely put a name to my face. They say to themselves, 'Hey, that's the girl from *Taxi*[33]'."

The icing on the cake: while the first episode had won over the public without convincing the critics, the press considers that this second opus proves to be "better than the original[34]", "Gérard Krawczyk's competent direction [being] strong with all the means at its disposal", says Jean-Jacques Bernard of the monthly *Première*[35]. Daniel must thus put the turbo into action to save the Japanese Minister of Defense, always flanked by Émilien, a young policeman who has failed his driving test many times.

----

32. Where the team of the film treads the famous red carpet in the mode "band of good friends" with Luc Besson, president of this 53rd edition.
33. *Télé-Poche*, n° 1787, May 2000.
34. *Studio Magazine, L'Année cinéma 2000*, special issue, December 2000.
35. *Première* n° 278, April 2000.

The film also includes some cult lines among young people. For example, Samy Naceri's answer when asked if he is a policeman: "No, I'm a trainee. I'm learning to regress."

If Marion Cotillard is not very visible in this film, this is voluntary:

> "I couldn't do any more because of my schedule. At the same time, I was shooting *Lisa*, a film by Pierre Grimblat, which had been planned for a long time. Luc Besson wrote my role as a wink[36]."

Marion Cotillard was awarded the Golden Swan for Best Actress of the Year for *Du bleu jusqu'en Amérique*, on June 18, 2000, at the 14th Cabourg Film Festival, which is mainly interested in romantic films. "An unforgettable adventure", according to our winner: "What I like in the cinema is to find myself in a room and go through all the states: laughter, tears, fear. It's the rare feeling, beyond love at first sight, that I felt when I read *From Blue to America*. I would have accepted any role in that story. Sometimes you read scripts where you love everything and would kill to make the movie! That's the case with *From the Blue to America*... And working with Sarah Lévy lived up to that feeling[37]."

36. *Télé-Poche*, n° 1787, May 8, 2000.
37. *Studio Magazine*, n° 151, December 1999.

Some time later, she got an important role in *Furia*, whose national release is set for August 9, 2000. It is the very first film of director Alexandre Aja, the son of Alexandre Arcady *(Le Grand Pardon, L'Union sacrée)*, then 20 years old, based on a short story by Julio Cortázar, *Graffiti*.

Marion Cotillard plays the role of Elia, a young girl tagging in a totalitarian world where writing on walls is punishable by death. Kidnapped by the authorities, she will suffer torture and the worst outrages, until a tragic end - her body is revealed in an anti-erotic way despite a rather torrid love scene with Stanislas Merhar. A role that allowed her to grow and gain confidence in herself.

> "Until *Furia*, I was learning my scenes and going into them without much prior thought. From then on, I learned to work upstream around my characters' imaginations, to spend more time with them[38]."

On the screen, the result is convincing.

> "The film is romantic, engaging and served by a very brave performance by Marion Cotillard. The torture scene - an explicit reference to *1984* - is a bravura piece. Unfortunately, *Furia* also has the flaws of youth: naivety and over-enthusiasm.

---

38. Interview by Thierry Chèze in *Studio Magazine*, n° 173, December 2001, p. 130-131.

> And by wanting to multiply the tracks too much, Aja loses the spectator. This confusion, added to a leaden soundtrack, is somewhat irritating. What remains is a promising direction, in the service of a genre little treated in our cinema[39]."

The film - forbidden to children under 12 - is set in a futuristic world ruled by a dictatorship in which the people resist by drawing on the walls. The low-budget film, shot in the former Portuguese city of El Jadida, south of Casablanca, did not meet with the expected success: 8,403 French spectators turned out for its release.

However, *Furia is* intriguing in *retrospect* when we know the fate linking Marion Cotillard and the eldest son of producer and director Claude Berri, Julien Rassam (Rassam being the name of his mother[40]), with whom she lived a passionate relationship.

"Who would have thought that their story would end in such a tragic way?" asks Claude Berri throughout the pages of his *Self-Portrait*[41] in which he evokes their love and then his most painful tragedy: "On October 18, 1998, Julien fell from the third

39. Comments by Sophie Benamon in *Studio Magazine*, n° 158, July-August 2000.
40. Anne-Marie Rassam, mother also of Thomas Langmann, actor-producer.
41. Claude BERRI, *Autoportrait*, Léo Scheer, Paris, 2003.

floor of the Raphael Hotel: a failed act or an almost successful suicide?" The question remains open, the tragic event occurring fourteen months after the death of his mother. Anne-Marie Rassam actually committed suicide by jumping from the ninth floor of the building of Augusta Emma Schweinberger (known as Gusti, the mother of Isabelle Adjani), in August 1997. In his book, Claude Berri can not help but expose himself completely, using these terrible words: "By dint of waiting for him, he had swallowed I do not know what crap and fell from a third floor window. A drama from which he came out alive, but quadriplegic. Marion will take a long time to recover, because they lived "a fusional love, intense and relentless[42]", according to a close to the actress.

Julien Rassam died on February 3, 2002, at the age of 33. "His heart must have given out after having absorbed so many toxic products", concludes his father, who does not want to believe that his son - manic-depressive - could have committed suicide or let himself die.

For *Furia*, his last film, Julien has only a secondary role - that of a resistance fighter - but he has played other characters before, including the lead role in Bruno Nuytten's *Albert souffre* in 1992, which is also the year of release of Claude Miller's *L'Accompagnatrice*, for which he is nominated for a

42. *Closer*, n° 143, March 10, 2008.

César for best male hopeful before getting the role of Alençon in Patrice Chéreau's *La Reine Margot* in 1994.

And then arises in Marion's career a real melodrama inspired by Patrick Cauvin's *Theatre in the Night*, which became *Lisa* under the direction of Pierre Grimblat[43]. According to the periods crossed in the film, the title role is sometimes played by Marion Cotillard, sometimes by the septuagenarian Jeanne Moreau, a great star of the big screen since the 1950s and then recently awarded the Best Actress prize for *The Old Woman Who Walked into the Sea* by Laurent Heynemann.

Lisa, released in theaters on January 10, 2001, shows a young contemporary filmmaker (Benoît Magimel) whose project is to make a short film about Sylvain Marceau (Sagamore Stévenin), a rising star of the 1940s, who disappeared in the turmoil of the war. His luck leads him to meet the woman who was his hero's great love, Lisa Maurin, who is still waiting for his return.

What did the press say?

"Here is a film like no one dares to make anymore. One of those romantic films that claim

---

43. Director of Slogan and also at the origin of the meeting between Serge Gainsbourg and Jane Birkin in May 1968. Lisa is his first film of fiction for the cinema since Say it with flowers in 1974.

their excesses, that accumulate all the traps, defy all the ridiculousness, dare everything with a curious mixture of innocence and boastfulness. One of these films that it will be easy to make fun of - cynics, prudish, trendy, dry hearts, abstain! - but which nevertheless, and precisely because of all that, will manage to ring true, and even, to draw us laughter and tears...

If we manage to get past the clichés, it is because the story is served by actors who also ring true and have each in their own way, accents of incredible truth and overwhelming emotions (Marion Cotillard, Jeanne Moreau - ah, her voice... -, Benoît Magimel, Sagamore Stévenin, Michel Jonasz)[44]."

However, here again, the reception was mixed: *Lisa* recorded only 43,970 admissions. Marion Cotillard has no reason to regret this film, in which her performance as a lover devoured by tuberculosis is admired and earned her the Best Actress Award at the 6th Schermi d'Amore[45] in Verona on April 29, 2001. It is also the opportunity for her to sing on screen with her elder *L'Homme d'amour,* former title of "the Moreau" with a voice of anthology. Jeanne sitting at the piano and Marion watching Benoît Magimel from behind her shoulder offer us a very moving moment:

44. Jean-Pierre Lavoignat in *Studio Magazine*, n° 163, January 2001.
45. Literally: "Écrans d'Amour". This festival is dedicated to melodrama in all its variations.

"For a waltz
With a man of love
So that he embraces me
Until the end of the day
I gave my life
I gave my heart
I gave myself and then, and then
There was sweetness
He left me and then, and then
That's why I cry
That's why I cry
[…]."

TIM BURTON[46]
AND *THE PRETTY THINGS*

If Marion Cotillard loves to sing, she offers to her public some delicious performances thanks to her deliciously broken voice. Thus, on November 7, 2000, for one of the key scenes of the film *Les Jolies Choses* by Gilles Paquet-Brenner, on the stage of the Zenith in Paris, she interprets, in the middle of the concert of Patrick Bruel, *La Fille de joie*[47].

> "It was a little girl's dream and a unique opportunity for me. I took lessons, but because everything happened so quickly, we had little time to prepare, the song itself was not recorded a few days before the day. I couldn't do it. But I was stung to the core when I was told that if I couldn't do it, we would use the voice of Axelle Renoir (who composed the melody)! I didn't want to find myself in front of 7,000 people and sing in playback on someone else's voice! So I did it and, when the

46. The American filmmaker Tim Burton was born in 1958. He is recognized as the master of fantasy in the new millennium and associated with the gothic movement since Edward Scissorhands in 1990.
47. Another title sung by Marion Cotillard in *Les Jolies Choses*: "La conne".

time came, I wasn't really afraid, because it wasn't me, but Marie who was on that stage. I wanted above all to have no regrets when I returned backstage. And I enjoyed every single one of those 240 seconds. It was magic to see the lighters lit, to play with the public. I really enjoyed it. It will remain an unforgettable memory[48]."

"Marion is a rare actress. She is very intense while managing to nuance. I'm not worried about her, she can play anything[49]", says Patrick Bruel.[50]

It is true. However, it is less known that after a "yes" in principle to the director - who chose her on the advice of a mutual friend, the actress Élodie Navarre - Marion Cotillard got scared and refused the (double) role.

"Lucie and Marie were too close to me. I was afraid to face things I didn't want to face[51]."

However, this film does not cease to haunt her.

"I was convinced that I had made a mistake. So I had my mother and a close friend read the script, and they definitely convinced me[52]."

---

48. Interview by Thierry Chèze in *Studio Magazine*, n° 173, December 2001, p. 130-131.
49. *Ibid.*
50. Playing Jacques in *Les Jolies Choses*.
51. Interview by Thierry Chèze, quoted article.
52. *Ibid.*

She calls back Paquet-Brenner and the adventure can then begin.

> In the end, "[Gilles Paquet-Brenner's] first film (which he adapted from Virginie Despentes' novel of the same name, "written in three or four days on coke"[53] according to the author), resembles its twin heroines: at first easy, a little flashy, it then turns out to be a little clumsy, confused, sometimes surly, then becomes attractive, seductive, exhilarating, disturbing, touching, and finally terribly likeable.
>
> In this double role of Marie and Julie, twin sisters, enemy sisters, plunged into the hell of show business, Marion Cotillard seems to reveal herself at last: she is breathtaking. Great actress, she did not miss this unique opportunity to play on a multitude of registers but also to sing! She deserves a César as well as a Victoire[54].

Thanks to this film, Marion Cotillard is a true personal success. Gilles Paquet-Brenner had already directed her last year in a medium-length film, *The Marquis*, before giving her this first major role. The antagonistic characters of Lucie F. and Marie, giving her the opportunity to offer two beautiful performances in opposite registers, lead her to receive a second nomination for the César of the best female

---

53. lemague.net, September 24, 2010.
54. Comments by Patrick Fabre in *Studio Magazine*, n° 173, December 2001.

hope. The answer came on March 2, 2002 at the Châtelet theater during the 27th Cesar ceremony, presided over by Nathalie Baye: the winner was finally Rachida Brakni - the favorite - for *Chaos* by Coline Serreau. This is the occasion for our heroine to be wished all the "nice things" in the world.

Admiringly, Marion Cotillard, who was then 26 years old, said of her elder Nathalie Baye:

> "I would love to shoot with her! I had the opportunity to meet her during a trip to India for Unifrance, and I fell under her spell. I find her career exemplary, if only because of the way she has returned to the forefront of the scene[55] and has since made herself indispensable. I love the simplicity that emanates from her. What could be more beautiful than an actress who knew how to stay real[56]?"

Released in theaters on November 14, 2001, with a ban on children under 12, *Les Jolies Choses*, although awarded the Michel d'Ornano Prize at the 27th Deauville American Film Festival on September 9, 2001, was a more than modest success since the number of admissions in France was 202,027.

---

55. In 1999, Nathalie Baye returned to success in theaters with *Venus Beauty (Institute)* by Tonie Marshall, after nine years without success and a little complicated.

56. "Les dix jeunes actrices françaises qu'on s'arrache", *Studio Magazine*, n° 215, September 2005.

This is very unfortunate for our actress, who is shooting *Taxi 3*, in Paris and Marseille.

On April 30, 2002, we find Marion Cotillard on the screens in Guillaume Nicloux's *Une affaire privée*, nicely supported by the critics in general and by *Studio Magazine* in particular:

> "Connoisseurs know that in the detective story, everything is a matter of style. And this *private affair is* not lacking in style. Guillaume Nicloux, who had left us a bit disappointed with his previous attempt (*Le Poulpe*, in 1998), succeeds this time in a well-balanced cocktail, with just the right amount of classicism and strangeness to make the viewer feel jubilant.
>
> At ease in this universe (Nicloux also writes thrillers), he also possesses a sense of ellipsis and a small irony of everyday life that calls for the viewer's complicity.
>
> Led by Thierry Lhermitte, astonishing in this role against the grain, and Marion Cotillard, generous of sensuality, supported by very typical supporting roles (Jeanne Balibar, Jean-Pierre Darroussin, Aurore Clément, etc.), *A Private Affair* finds the right tone between homage to the noir series and originality. Of course, we can regret a small weakness in the denouement of the plot (a little too simple), but really no reason to sulk our pleasure[57]."

57. Christophe D'YVOIRE, *Studio Magazine,* n° 177, April 2002.

In this classic and strange thriller, Marion Cotillard plays Clarisse, a young girl who develops a romantic relationship with François Manéri, a private investigator looking for her best friend, Rachel Siprien, who has been missing for six months.

Unfortunately, at the time when *Les Bronzés*[58] made their return to the big screen with a full house, the public followed only modestly. Thierry Lhermitte - 50 years old that year - is therefore shunned while the role of the disillusioned detective in *A Private Affair* is one of the most valuable of his career - this film could have been his own *Tchao Pantin*[59].

Thus, with 458,565 admissions, *Une affaire privée is* somewhat disappointing despite the Diane and Lucien Barrière Foundation's Cinema Prize, which rewards a new talent in the person of Guillaume Nicloux.

Cab 3 brings Marion Cotillard back to the top of the box office with Samy Naceri[60] and Frédéric Diefenthal, who (re)establish the classic comedy

58. Patrice Leconte's film that undoubtedly launched in 1978 the Splendid band, composed of Thierry Lhermitte playing Popeye, pectoral in the wind and hitting on chicks "à la balance".
59. This film by Claude Berri totaled nearly 4 million admissions with Coluche, who won the Best Actor award in 1984.
60. Following his "bloodshed", it begins to be said that he is the new enfant terrible of French cinema: the newspapers talk a lot about his problems with the law.

tandem. This time, Daniel and Emilien are confronted with a mysterious rollerblading gang whose members - in reality, dangerous Chinese - are wearing Santa Claus costumes.

We find them on January 29, 2003 on the screens of France, with, for the second time at the controls, Gérard Krawczyk passing the third. As a *guest star*, we find Sylvester Stallone, then 56 years old. In spite of a certain slowdown compared to the last opus, the film nevertheless became the leader for the year 2003, with 6.1 million admissions (a respectable score even though it was the lowest of the three parts).

Despite the many detractors of the saga and the success of the film, Luc Besson and Gerard Krawczyk must, it seems, deliver a *Taxi 4*. This will be the case in 2007, but without Marion Cotillard because, for the time being, "the Cotillard" in the making sees red. Indeed, if she does not forget that the first episode of *Taxi* gave her the opportunity to meet the public, now our actress faces obstacles: people in the business are somewhat shunning her because of her recurring role in the series of Luc Besson. Thus, the role has confined her, in the eyes of "professionals of the profession" in the image of a midinette (except Gilles Paquet-Brenner with *Les Jolies Choses*, the work is however very confidential).

If the refusals hurt Marion, this difficult period is also due to her requirement. Marion works according to two parameters: not only must the role suit her, but also that the film is a beautiful project. So, to deserve quality films, she leaves her character of Lilly, daughter of General Bertineau in the *Taxi* trilogy. Our actress does not want to be satisfied with what is offered to her and aspires to more powerful roles. Let Luc Besson say it: Marion Cotillard has the will to change register!

> "Let's be honest: I'm being replaced in *Taxi*, it doesn't change anything. What I'm doing in it isn't kicking ass on the floor, but it's pretty sweet. People didn't think, "This girl is amazing." But they also didn't think, "She sucks, bye"[61] !"

Thus, if Marion Cotillard does not doubt her talent, she almost stopped everything.

> "I didn't want to wait, to be unhappy, to watch sublime roles go by that I didn't have access to and to become bitter[62]."

That's what I said, with an open heart. As a result, she is thinking of devoting her energy to

61. "La Môme Cotillard", *Première*, n° 356, October 2006.
62. "Marion Cotillard: our absolute icon," *Glamour*, No. 100, July 2012.

doing something else entirely and is considering working with Greenpeace[63]:

> "At that point, I felt like I belonged with them.
> And then just as I told my agent I was quitting,
> I got a role in Tim Burton's *Big Fish*[64]."

Marion Cotillard flew on January 6, 2003 to Alabama, where she will stay for two months to shoot under the direction of a filmmaker she worships[65]. She plays the role of the young French wife of William Bloom (Billy Crudup), who goes to the bedside of her dying father (Albert Finney) to unravel the mysteries of his life. Ewan McGregor plays this father figure in his youth while Jessica Lange plays his wife.

63. An international environmental non-governmental organization, founded in 1971 and headquartered in Amsterdam, the Netherlands.
64. "Marion Cotillard: our absolute icon," *Glamour*, No. 100, July 2012.
65. It is then the tenth feature film of Tim Burton since Pee-Wee Big Adventure in 1985.

GUILLAUME CANET
AND *JEUX D'ENFANTS*

Rich of her American experience, Marion Cotillard returns to France with the film *Jeux d'enfants* by Yann Samuell, the actress[66] planned for the role of Sophie Kowalski decided to withdraw from the project. For this first feature film, Yann Samuell auditioned 70 actresses, including Marion Cotillard. It was only a month and a half later that she received an answer after several attempts with Guillaume Canet - the latter having done everything possible to prevent her from getting the role, in vain! "I wanted it too much![67]," says Marion Cotillard, who, for her part, had expressed her interest in the film to the director as soon as she read the script.

> "But once we arrived on the set," Guillaume Canet assures us, "we quickly had a lot of fun together. This complicity was very useful to make the romantic situations we had to play credible[68]."

66. Virginie Ledoyen.
67. *Studio Magazine*, n° 192, September 2003.
68. *Ibid*.

During the first days of shooting, Marion Cotillard was not subject to stage fright with Guillaume Canet. An important preliminary work with Yann Samuell made their communication ideal, so much so that she affirms: "In the restaurant scene, where Guillaume's character pretends to ask me to marry him, I even surprised myself, at the moment of the "Cut!", for a few seconds, not to realize that we were shooting a film. It's a very pleasant feeling to be caught up in this exchange[69].

But the first meeting between the two actors, now considered the standard-bearers of the young generation of French cinema, did not take place at the time of testing and shooting of the film - started in May 2002[70]. In truth, it goes back to 1996, on the set of Coline Serreau's *La Belle Verte*, on which Guillaume Canet had come to join a friend, the actress Claire Keim. Then "we saw each other a lot since then, but we did not really know each other before starting the film[71]," concludes Marion Cotillard. For the record, they were both nominated for the 1999 César for Best

69. *Ibid.*
70. At that time, on May 21, 2002, alongside Clotilde Courau, Marion Cotillard with a gothic tendency climbed the steps of the Palais du Festival de Cannes for the premiere of the film Sweet Sixteen by Ken Loach.
71. *Studio Magazine*, n° 192, September 2003.

Newcomer - she for *Taxi*; he for *En plein cœur*, by Pierre Jolivet (the winner being Bruno Putzulu for the role of Lionel in *Petits désordres amoureux* by Olivier Péray).

Then 30 years old, Guillaume Canet[72] had, since his debut in the cinema, multiplied the meetings with some of the greatest names of the French seventh art, from Jean Rochefort - for his first role in *Barracuda*, released in 1997 - to Gérard Depardieu - in *Vidocq*, in 2001. And, of course, he tried his hand at Hollywood in 2000 with *The Beach*, in which he played alongside Leonardo DiCaprio. But, having always decided to move on to directing, he took advantage of the opportunity to make his mark with a few short films and commercials. *My Idol*, released in December 2002, is a scathing fable that addresses, with a wry sense of humor, the themes of power, ambition, corruption: Guillaume Canet is both co-producer, director, co-writer and actor. In this last film, his wife Diane Kruger (since September 2001) is the main actress.

With *Jeux d'enfants*, we have in front of us a real cinema couple. "These two are going to love each other, that's for sure", we say to ourselves, although the perverse and now famous game of "course or

72. Guillaume Canet was born on April 10, 1973, in Boulogne-Billancourt in the Hauts-de-Seine.

no course" that Yann Samuell imposes on Sophie[73] and Julien[74], is not to simplify their task. However, he offers the two actors one of the richest roles of their young careers:

> "By turns funny, seductive, astonishing, upsetting, they have here the possibility to change register in the blink of an eye, to build characters over time, to play the depth and the multitude of feelings. A godsend for them. A joy for us[75]."

Jeux d'enfants is one of the biggest successes of 2003, having passed the symbolic million spectator mark. On the occasion of the release of the film, scheduled for September 17, 2003, when *Gala*[76] asks her to evoke her "first meeting with her lover", Marion Cotillard replied: "It was five years ago... Wonderful!"

Marion Cotillard remains discreet about her relationship with Stéphan Guérin-Tillié. Already,

73. Sophie at 8 years old is interpreted by Josephine Lebas-Joly, and otherwise interpreted at 80 years old by Nathalie Nattier, who, in 1946, replaced Marlene Dietrich in Marcel Carné's *Les Portes de la nuit*, for better or for worse..., and whose Jeux d'enfants is her first film since 1959! In addition, it was she who managed to get Roger Willar, her husband in the city, hired...
74. Julien at 8 years old is interpreted by Thibault Verhaeghe, and otherwise interpreted at 80 years old by Robert Willar, one of the historical voices of Europe 1.
75. Patrick FABRE, *Studio Magazine*, n° 192, September 2003.
76. *Gala*, n° 535, September 10, 2003.

in April 2000, Thierry Ardisson, during the program *Tout le monde en parle*[77], asked her insistently about her "prince charming, actor and director, met a year and a half ago" without naming him. This being so, to the question "First "I love you"?", Jeanne Bordes received as an answer: "I was 20 years old. He lived in Belgium. And it is my first and only love at first sight[78]."

Period!

Guillaume Canet and Marion Cotillard embody the young French generation full of desire, hope, motivation and, clearly, a future. *Jeux d'enfants was* also a respectable success internationally, under the title, *Love me if you dare*. On April 25, 2004, at the 7th American Film Festival in Newport Beach, it was awarded the prize for best dramatic film. The same festival awarded Marion Cotillard the prize for best dramatic actress.

Two months later, at Disneyland Paris, the couple Canet-Cotillard is rewarded with the NRJ Ciné Award for the best "kiss" while the film is also awarded for the best "ending".

A good omen for them and particularly for Marion Cotillard, who received on May 14, 2004 - with the Brazilian Rodrigo Santoro (known in

---

77. Date of the program on April 22, 2010 on France 2.
78. *Gala*, n° 535, September 10, 2003.

particular for his interpretation in *Love Actually*) - the trophy Revelation Chopard /Studio *Magazine*, rewarding young actors noticed worldwide. The trophy was presented to her by Laura Morante at the 57th Cannes Film Festival, where Marion Cotillard met Diane Kruger (the previous winner) and Guillaume Canet on the Croisette.

If the young Frenchwoman is no longer a revelation in the strict sense of the word - since she made her debut in 1994 and became known to the general public thanks to *Taxi* - it is truly with *Children's Games* and *Big Fish* that she was able to show the greatest number of people the extent of her talent and her acting - in particular an aptitude, rarer than it seems, for fantasy.

Released in France on March 3, 2004, *Big Fish* allows him to cross the universe of Tim Burton, still popular in France (1.1 million admissions), with an infinite sweetness. The director signs one of his most personal films, a cocktail of enchantment and realism that reveals his interrogations as a filmmaker and an unprecedented maturity.

A Cesar

The quality is not measured by the number of scenes, and his thousand and one facets shone, with a vengeful rage, in *Un long dimanche de fiançailles* (based on the novel by Sébastien Japrisot). A prestigious film with 4.4 million viewers in France. It's an understatement to say that its director, Jean-Pierre Jeunet, was expected to make a big splash after the colossal success of The *Fabulous Destiny of Amélie Poulain*, released in April 2001 - whose candid freshness of the title character is expressed through the petulant Audrey Tautou. Nevertheless, three and a half years later, Jeunet continues to surprise critics:

> "Inhabited by Audrey Tautou who, like the filmmaker, digs deeper into the furrow opened by Amélie..., carried as always by an original and formidable cast in every way, this film is a fascinating puzzle, of a warm, fraternal and moving humanity[79]."

79. Jean-Pierre LAVOIGNAT, *Studio Magazine*, n° 206, November 2004.

As we see, 2004 is a pivotal year for the career of Marion Cotillard, which did not seem to want to take off. Also for her interpretation of Tina Lombardi, a prostitute seeking to avenge the death of her husband during the First World War, she will get, from the hands of Richard Berry, the Cesar[80] for best supporting actress, at the expense of Ariane Ascaride *(Brodeuses)*, Mylène Demongeot *(36, quai des Orfèvres)*, Julie Depardieu *(Podium)* and Émilie Dequenne *(L'Équipier)*. On February 26, 2005 at the Châtelet, during the 30th ceremony of the César presided by Isabelle Adjani, Marion Cotillard seems filled with joy when she says she loves her job:

> "The César still allowed me to know that the way people in the profession looked at me was changing[81]."

From now on, the scripts come in number and it is with an avowed greed that Marion will make a series of films: during 2005, she will appear in six films more or less commensurate with her talent: *Innocence*, by Lucile Hadzihalilovic; *Cavalcade*, by Steve Suissa; *Ma vie en l'air*, by Rémi Bezançon;

---

80. Out of 12 nominations, *Un long dimanche de fiançailles* received five César awards: male hope (Gaspard Ulliel), photography (Bruno Delbonnel), costumes (Madeline Fontaine) and set design (Aline Bonetto), as well as the César for best supporting actress.
81. *Madame Figaro*, n° 1104, 22 October 2005.

La Boîte noire, by Richard Berry; *Edy*, by Stéphan Guérin-Tillié and *Mary*, by Abel Ferrara.

Innocence, the first of them, was released on January 12, 2005. It follows 35 prepubescent girls who learn dance and natural sciences in a strange school, forbidden to men and isolated in the middle of a forest.

In this film - based on a short story by Frank Wedekind, *Mine-Haha of the corporal education of young girls*, written in 1888 and transposed in the 1960s for its adaptation to the big screen - Marion Cotillard plays, with Hélène de Fougerolles, one of the two mysterious teachers, opposite Corinne Marchand (the director) made famous by Agnès Varda's cult film, *Cléo de 5 à 7* (1962). Although these are secondary roles, it is above all to reassure some investors that the young filmmaker has hired both. Lucile Hadzihalilovic had then thought:

> "Both have an image of modern girls but I think they have a classic face, a little out of time, which corresponded well to the universe of the film. I also wanted them to be very pretty and feminine[82].

---

82. allocine.fr

Today, his first feature film remains an undeserved failure (with only 8,541 admissions) in view of the awards he has received here and there, including the Spanish Prize for Best New Director at the 52nd San Sebastian Film Festival 2004, the Swedish Bronze Horse for Best Film at the 15th Stockholm Film Festival 2004, the Japanese Special Jury Prize at the 16th Yubari Fantastic Film Festival 2005, the Fipresci Prize and the Turkish Audience Prize at the 24th Istanbul Film Festival 2005, or the 21st Very Special Prize, consecrating the most singular film of the year, on June 8th 2005.

Cavalcade, which will be released in France on May 25, 2005, introduces Marion Cotillard as Alizée, who urges her partner, a night owl, to change his lifestyle if he does not want to live alone. So, after a few days of reflection, Léo leaves in his car to join her and is the victim of an accident that renders him a quadriplegic.

The film is adapted from the autobiographical bestseller by Bruno de Stabenrath, with the unexpected Titoff in the main role (remember that the comedian has already played his lover, Sebastien, in *Les Jolies Choses*). On February 23, 2006, for his role in *Cavalcade*, Titoff was nominated for the Gérard[83]

---

83. Arthur Jugnot (son of Gérard Jugnot, born in 1980, present in Cavalcade) is, as for him, the winner of the worst actor or actress "son of or daughter of".

for the Worst Actor, which went to Michaël Youn for *Iznogoud*, by Patrick Braoudé. In 2007, during the 2nd satirical ceremony, he was the winner of the Gérard for the Worst Actor or Director of 2005 who did not shoot in 2006.

On the other hand, Marion Cotillard has created a real suspense about her "friendly participation" in Steve Suissa's film[84]. He tells it himself:

> "I sent her a script in New York where she was shooting Tim Burton's *Big Fish*. It took her a while to respond, so I thought she wasn't interested. But ten days before the shoot she called me to ask when she was starting[85]."

With only 87,762 admissions, the film that was described as "frankly disappointing, but saved from the wreckage by the performance of Marion Cotillard[86]" did not receive the honors of the French public.

Ma vie en l'air, starring Marion Cotillard with Vincent Elbaz and Gilles Lellouche, premiered (out of competition) at the 19th Cabourg Film Festival and was released on September 7, 2005.

---

84. Straight out of the Cours Florent, Steve Suissa had previously directed (unsuccessfully) two feature films, *L'Envol* (2000) and *Le Grand Rôle* (2004), before becoming a recognized theater director.
85. allocine.fr
86. *Ciné-Télé-Revue*, n° 22, June 2, 2005.

It is the first film of Rémi Bezançon, then 34 years old.

> "However, it presents us with sympathetic cha-racters, interpreted by a fresh and enthusiastic cast. Consensual? Certainly. But funny. Isn't that what you want from a comedy[87]?"

During the run of this romantic comedy, 400,488 French viewers followed Yann (Vincent Elbaz), an airline employee, as he recounts the joys and sorrows caused by his fear of flying, which prevented him from following his fiancée halfway around the world in his youth. The day Alice (Marion Cotillard), a relationship counselor on a radio station, moves in next door to him, his life is totally changed.

While Gilles Lellouche was nominated for the 2006 César for Best Newcomer[88] for the role of Ludo, Marion Cotillard was nominated for the Crystal Globe for Best Actress[89].

For eleven years, we have seen her expand the field of possibilities without ever being locked into a specific job, to become one of the key figures of French cinema. The heroine of *Ma vie en l'air* found herself in front of Ridley Scott's camera, opposite Russell Crowe, for *A Good Year*. Over the films and

87. Augustin ARRIVÉ, *Studio Magazine*, n° 215, September 2005.
88. Winner Louis Garrel for *Les Amants réguliers* by Philippe Garrel.
89. Winner Nathalie Baye for *Le Petit Lieutenant* by Xavier Beauvois.

roles, her range of play has continued to grow and assert itself. Marion Cotillard will then embark on a major project. She confirmed to Michel Drucker, on the set of *Vivement dimanche*, that she will play Edith Piaf in a film by Olivier Dahan. "I have the impression of being at the bottom of Everest but I will climb it," she promised on the famous red sofa of the presenter of France 2.

And how!

Magazines are now interested in the sentimental life of the actress, including the weekly magazine *Voici*, which reveals to the general public her romance with Sinclair[90], a series of stolen photos to support it. "In mid-March, he went for a weekend in Marrakech with the actress Marion Cotillard and since then, he spends a lot of time at her place," informs us on page 14 the journalist Sophie Desville in the edition No. 911 of April 25, 2005, with the following headline: "Marion Cotillard with Sinclair! The musician has separated from Emma de Caunes". The magazine reiterated his words in the issue 933 of September 26, 2005, with the following headline: "Emma de Caunes /

---

90. Sinclair (who already signed the soundtrack of the film *Mon Idole*) is the author of the soundtrack of Ma vie en l'air.

Sinclair: they divorce[91]". He does not leave Marion Cotillard...

A commercial feat.

More glamorous, the women's magazine *Elle honors* her for the first time in its No. 3098 dated May 16, 2005, with this statement: "Marion Cotillard, the passion of the game." She then shares the cover of the monthly *Studio Magazine* No. 215 of September 2005 with Ludivine Sagnier, the favorite actress of François Ozon[92] to then continue its "irresistible rise" on the front page of *Madame Figaro*, October 22, 2005 No. 19041.

Thus, Marion Cotillard tends to impose herself as much in the world of French cinema as well as in the great family of the French press. A new star is born!

> "Fame is not a cure for anything. Fame only gets me great scripts and makes great movies. Anecdotally, fame can get me a seat in a crowded restaurant, which I don't care about anyway, it also makes people nice when they pass me, when I go to buy a loaf of bread. Above all, thanks to it, I can push doors to meet beautiful people, interesting people with whom I want to go for a while

91. The couple Emma de Caunes / Sinclair married on September 15, 2001, they are the parents of a little Nina, born in October 2002.
92. *Gouttes d'eau sur pierres brûlantes* (2000), *8 femmes* (2002) and *Swimming pool* (2003).

to tell stories. But this is by no means the key to happiness[93]."

On September 30, 2005, Marion Cotillard is 30 years old.

According to Honoré de Balzac, this age constitutes a peak in a woman's existence. Indeed, despite her childlike face, it is a milestone for the actress who arrives at the age where everyone draws up a first balance sheet of his life course:

> "I thought not so long ago that 30 was just lurking around the corner and that it was a deadline that seemed hypothetical all together. Suddenly, it's here. And it brings me face to face with certain realities that I will have to take into account: I am not married, I have no children. But I needed to get my foot in the door of this profession, I wouldn't have been able to invest in a family life without having accomplished my dreams, I wouldn't have been able to manage this frustration, it would have been too painful, as much for me as for those around me[94].

The Black Box, by Richard Berry, will be released in theaters on November 2, 2005. After an offbeat comedy about love[95] and a tender film about

93. *Madame Figaro* n° 1104, October 22, 2005.
94. *Madame Figaro*, n° 1104, 22 October 2005.
95. *The (Delicate) Art of Seduction*, released in 2000.

childhood[96], he now tackles a psychological thriller by adapting a short story of the same name by Tonino Benacquista about brotherhood and guilt. This may be an (unconscious) allusion to his relationship with his sister, Marie, which he recently revealed on the front page of *Paris Match* No. 2935 of August 18, 2005.

> "It is the story of a man, Arthur Seligman (José Garcia), who, victim of a car accident, loses part of his memory. Isabelle, a nurse, whom I play, watched over him and noted in a notebook everything he said during the awakening phase that followed his coma. It remains for Arthur to reconstitute a puzzle with increasingly disturbing perspectives as the pieces fall into place... I was fascinated by this plunge into the unconscious of an individual, I met Richard, he spoke to me of this adventure with such ardor and enthusiasm that I was immediately excited. For me, to enter into the adventure of a film, it is essential to feel that the director is literally inhabited by his story[97].

About the actress, Richard Berry is full of praise: "Marion Cotillard is a gift. She is an actress I love. She is exciting, beautiful, human[98].

---

96. *Me César, 10 ½ years old, 1 m 39,* released in 2003.
97. *Madame Figaro,* n° 1104, 22 October 2005.
98. *Ibid.*

If the public responds (477,444 admissions), *The Black Box* is nevertheless nominated for the Gérard for the Worst Film (winner *Iznogoud*, by Patrick Braoudé) and José Garcia wins the Gérard for the Worst Attempt of a Comedian in a Dramatic Role "à la Coluche in *Tchao Pantin*" (winner Élie Semoun in *Aux abois*, by Philippe Collin)

Edy, also released on November 2, 2005, is Stéphan Guérin-Tillié's first feature film. After ten years of experience as an actor on a set, he wanted to write and tell his own stories, after making two short films: *J'ai fait des sandwiches pour la route* (1999) and *Requiem(s)* (2001). The story of *Edy is* a novelty for François Berléand, who is not used to lead roles. The actor was already present in his short film *Requiem(s)*. The director does not know if he would have made it without him.

The film deals with the misadventures of an insurance agent, raised in an unorthodox way by Louis (played by Philippe Noiret, whose penultimate film is).[99]

Stéphan Guérin-Tillié also wrote this crime comedy with Marion Cotillard in mind, whom he has known for a very long time. They have in common two short films, *Quelques jours de trop* (2000)

99. Philippe Noiret died on November 23, 2006, at the age of 76 years. 3 friends of Michel Boujenah, is his last film. It was released in 2007.

and *Heureuse* (2001), an episode of the series *Les Redoutables* (2001, episode *Doggy Dog*), and, more recently, the film *Cavalcade*[100].

Let us note also, that they were together in the life. It was through her that he met Frederic Bourboulon, the producer of *Edy*. "Once my script was finished, I sent it to him. Marion, who had accepted the role and worked with him on *A Private Affair* (2001), added a little note saying that she would be happy if Frédéric read it. And, three weeks later, Frédéric called me[101].

"When I read his script, I was blown away by the originality of the story, by the dialogues, which are worthy of a Michel Audiard. In addition, Stéphan has an extremely personal visual universe. As a result, his film has a real personality, which is not so common[102].

"Marion is the actress of my life", says Stéphan Guérin-Tillié (33) in the press kit of the film...

> "And for me, the most singular actress of her generation. She is rare as Romy Schneider could be. They have in common this same flaw, these moments of total abandonment. One can only be in love with her as with Romy Schneider.

100. Stéphan Guérin-Tillié plays the role of Mickey.
101. cinemotions.com 2005, excerpt from the film's press kit.
102. *Madame Figaro* n° 1104, October 22, 2005.

I couldn't imagine anyone else in this role. Her two scenes are short but complicated because, in the end, she embodies a kind of icon, the feminine ideal in a way.

It must be inscribed in turn in the dream and in reality, without losing a phantasmatic aspect.

Marion has these two dimensions both in her acting and in her presence. She can be of a striking beauty, very femme fatale, and then become totally natural without artifice while keeping her magic. The scene between François Berléand and her gave rise to a moment of grace on the set. Like love at first sight between two people[103]."

Unfortunately, it is indifference for this offbeat thriller, with black humor. With 12,042 admissions, *Edy* went unnoticed in theaters.

Since then, Stéphan Guérin-Tillié, who was spotted as an actor in the film *Quatre Garçons pleins d'avenir* (1997), then in the TV film *Juste une question d'amour*[104], has not directed any more films or short films.

Mary was released in France on December 21, 2005, after having competed on September 6 of the same year at the 62nd Venice Film Festival - where it won the Jury's Special Grand Prize -, and

103. cinemotions.com 2005, excerpt from the film's press kit.
104. Where he played Cedric, who fell in love with a boy named Laurent, played by Cyrille Thouvenin. Broadcast on January 26, 2000 on France 2, Juste une question d'amour was seen by 6.3 million viewers.

since then in various festivals, including Deauville on September 9, 2005.

This is perhaps the most personal film by Abel Ferrara *(Bad Lieutenant, Our Funeral)*, who at 53 has a solid reputation as a provocative and subversive filmmaker. Shot at breakneck speed (four weeks between New York, Rome and Jerusalem), this is a low-budget production for the New York film-maker (4 million euros), with Juliette Binoche (41) as the central figure. She plays an actress incarnating Mary Magdalene and remains illuminated by this character. Discovering the film late, Juliette Binoche was positively shocked by it.

According to Abel Ferrara, *Mary* is his answer to Mel Gibson's *The Temptation of Christ*, the surprise hit of 2004. But Ferrara himself admits that he would never have been able to mount his project (which he had in mind for seven years) without the triumph of the previous one: 1.5 million admissions in France for *The Temptation of Christ* (with the Italian actress Monica Bellucci in the role of Mary Magdalene) against only 65,454 for *Mary*.

As for Marion Cotillard, who never meets Juliette Binoche in the film, she plays the role of a friend of Forrest Whitaker and Heather Graham. The couple will be confronted, in the city of New York, with a number of tests, and revelations, which will alternately make them doubt or believe in the existence of God. Even if it is a second role, her participation confirms that she now turns with the greatest. She has worked with Russell Crowe, under the direction of Ridley Scott for the film *A Good Year*[105], which was shot in Provence.

Let us recall that Marion Cotillard interpreted for the very first time the role of *Joan of Arc at the stake*[106], in an intense and moving way, on May 5 and 6, 2005 at the Palais des Sports in Orléans, during a concert given by the Orléans Symphony Orchestra under the direction of Jean-Marc Cochereau[107]. "The 3,000 spectators at the Palais des Sports still remember it. Just like the musicians and singers who participated in these two concerts[108]", says Catherine Mounier, the administrator of the Orleans Symphony Orchestra. "She interpreted Joan of Arc with what characterizes her talent: the ability to convey an immense emotion[109]", notes the conductor Jean-Marc Cochereau.

---

105. This American-British production was shot from August 29 to November 5, 2005.
106. Dramatic oratorio by Arthur Honegger on a libretto by Paul Claudel - whose French premiere was given in Orleans on May 8, 1939, with Ida Rubinstein in the role of Joan of Arc.
107. Christophe Maltot was then Brother Dominique.
108. lepoint.fr, March 27, 2008.
109. *Ibid.*

The actress' mother, Niseema Theillaud, had already interpreted *Joan of Arc at the stake*[110], in 1992, also directed by Jean-Marc Cochereau. Sitting in the front row in the cathedral of Orléans, Marion, 17 years old, had not lost a crumb of this show which marked her very much.

> "The last time I saw my mother work was in the cathedral in Orleans. She played *Joan of Arc at the stake*. Last year, she was called to take over the role. She answered that it was better to solicit me. She knew that it would be a blast for me. Her approach resembled a passing of the baton, a transmission[111]."

For Marion Cotillard, this oratorio is one of her most extraordinary experiences.

---

110. It was his father, Jean-Claude Cotillard, who played the role of Brother Dominique.
111. "La Môme Cotillard", *Première*, n° 356, October 2006.

LA MÔME

The year 2006 is marked by the beginning of the adventure of *La Môme*. It is because of her small meter forty-seven that Édith Piaf was nicknamed. The shooting of the biopic directed by Olivier Dahan began in Prague on January 16, for four and a half months. However, the preparation of the film began in September. Marion Cotillard plays the famous French singer, in a film that traces her exceptional destiny, from her childhood to fame, from Belleville to New York and until her last days. Piaf was 47 years old at the time but strongly marked by the years: Piaf is a thousand lives in one.

"Two years ago, my agent, Laurent Grégoire, told me that Olivier Dahan was preparing a film on the life of Edith Piaf and was thinking of me to play her. But it was only at the beginning of 2005 that I met Olivier, who told me about his project and gave me the script. Before reading it, I didn't know Piaf's life in detail. At one time, I listened to a lot of French realist songs, but Fréhel, Mistinguett and Yvette Guilbert as much as her. On the other hand, I had already "used" her songs to prepare roles, like the one I played in *Lisa*. So I opened this script without any preconceived

> ideas. And I devoured the 250 pages. I discovered the incredible richness of this woman's journey, marked by immense happiness and the most terrible dramas[112]…"

The role could have been played by Audrey Tautou, but Olivier Dahan would have, according to Marion Cotillard, detected "a similarity of [his] look with that of Edith Piaf[113]." The director finds that the latter has a temperament of tragedy. It will be Marion and no one else. From then on, the actress worked tirelessly, immersed herself body and soul in the role, devoured all the biographies of Piaf, including those of her lovers.

He will be joined by Jean-Pierre Martins as Marcel Cerdan, Jean-Paul Rouve[114] and Clotilde Courau as Piaf's parents, Catherine Allégret as her paternal grandmother, Gérard Depardieu as Louis Leplée (a cabaret director who discovered Edith Piaf), Sylvie Testud as Mômone, her best friend. Pascal Greggory played her manager, Caroline Silhol as Marlene Dietrich, and Emmanuelle Seigner as Titine, the resident of a brothel. The release of *La Môme is* scheduled for February 14, 2007.

---

112. *Studio Magazine*, n° 225, July/August 2006.
113. directmatin. r, 24 August 2013.
114. The name of Vincent Cassel had been announced to interpret the father of Edith Piaf as a child.

Before this date, Marion Cotillard appears in four feature films: *Sauf le respect que je vous dois* (February 15), *Toi et Moi* (March 8), *Dikkenek* (June 21) and *Fair Play* (September 6).

The first one, With all *due respect*[115], has him starring alongside Olivier Gourmet, Dominique Blanc and Julie Depardieu.

Warmly applauded on October 2, 2005 at the 7th edition of the Festival of European Cinema in Essonne (Cinessonne), this first film by Fabienne Godet was awarded the Audience Prize.

For her first feature film, which deals with the consequences of a dismissal, the filmmaker was inspired by her own professional experience in a hospital - where she worked on accompanying the dying. Pure realism not being the object of the film, it was more a matter of reporting the questions that this experience provoked in Fabienne Godet: why, and above all how do we accept the unacceptable, again and again, including the little things of daily life? What arrangements are we capable of in order to tolerate what we consider morally intolerable? What makes an individual freely submit to someone he or she does not even respect?

---

115. *Sauf le respect que je vous dois* is also the title of a song by Georges Brassens, dating from 1972.

In the film, Olivier Gourmet plays the role of a man[116] whose life is turned upside down when his friend (played by Jean-Michel Portal) commits suicide, victim of the moral harassment of their boss (Jean-Marie Winling). This film allowed Olivier Gourmet to win the Interpretation Award at the 9th Shanghai International Film Festival on June 25, 2006 and, for Fabienne Godet, the Best Director Award. Nevertheless, this very entertaining drama, which, without pretension or moral lessons, tells us: "Enough!" (which also won the Grand Jury Prize 2006[117] at the 8th Miami Film Festival) only attracted 110,449 French viewers. A true cry of anger, this film lets us see a, Marion Cotillard playing Lisa, a young woman on the fringe.

The director talks about this singular character:

> "Lisa is inspired by two or three people who are close to me, people who are deeply alive and free because they know they are mortal; not in an intellectual way but viscerally. They have the energy of those who know that time is short and do not make a big deal of it. What is important to them is to live a "living" life and they will always refuse to be locked into anything. In this sense, Lisa is the indispensable complement of François. He remained for a long time prisoner of his fear. She, on the other hand, goes for it [...] I like this

---

116. François in the film.
117. Ex aequo with Anklaget by Jacob Thuesen.

kind of people, a little bit on the fringe, because I believe that they hold a truth. They have a privileged point of view on the world[118].

Toi et Moi, directed by Julie Lopes-Curval (Caméra d'Or Cannes 2002 for *Bord de mer*, her first film), shows us the love affairs of Ariane (Julie Depardieu[119]), a writer of photo novels for the magazine *Toi et Moi*. She is sometimes inspired by the life of her sister Léna (Marion Cotillard), a very shy cellist - although she has two men in her life. Ariane, on the other hand, is still looking for Prince Charming. The critics have mixed feelings about this romantic comedy:

> "After *Bord de mer*, a brilliant but sometimes too staid exercise in style, Julie Lopes-Curval signs a second feature film full of deliciously kitschy still images that comment on the action with an old-fashioned irony[120]."

You and Me thus totaled 111,781 entries.

According to Julie Lopes-Curval, Marion Cotillard invested herself fully in the role of Lena

---

118. allocine.fr.
119. Daughter of Gérard Depardieu, "sacred monster" of French cinema *(Les Valseuses, Le Dernier Métro, Cyrano de Bergerac)...* Julie Depardieu (born in 1973) became the first actress to win two César awards for the same role: Best Newcomer and Best Supporting Actor for Claude Miller's La Petite Lili, in February 2004.
120. Isab*Elle* DANEL, *Première*, n° 349, March 2006.

by learning the cello. She worked entire nights to ensure the placement of her hand and know her score. She is doing well. "I like roles where I have to learn something, like the cello for *You and Me*[121]..."

As for the third film, *Dikkenek*[122], Mathieu Carratier's words summarize it as follows:

> "They're ugly, Belgian and mean, stealing cars, having threesomes and beating up children. They are "dikkenek", loudmouths who drive turbocharged BMWs and rush to the *peep show* as soon as it gets dark. They are uninhibited, ruthless and unscripted. This is the major flaw of this first feature film, which follows on from each other with the only thread being a frank and viral desire to make people laugh. On that level, no problem: with its gallery of energetic people with moustaches, *Dikkenek* deploys enough humor to take your lungs out. François Damiens, with a little sweat on his forehead and an injected eye, confirms that he is the funniest thing Belgium has produced since Benoît Poelvoorde. The rest of the cast is in unison. So *don't* be shocked, have a *pintje* and go see this little film that tastes exceedingly good[123]."

121. *Studio Magazine*, n° 231, February 2007.
122. Pronounce "Diquenèque". This is the Brussels expression for a "fat neck", the French equivalent of a pretentious or boastful person.
123. Mathieu Carratier, *Première*, n° 353, July 2006.

In 1995, then almost a beginner in cinema (she had only made her first feature film the year before), Marion Cotillard played the lead role in Olivier Van Hoofstadt's first short film: *Snuff Movie*. Eleven years later, she answered present for the first feature film of the Belgian director who wrote for her, this time, the hilarious role of Nadine, an unusual teacher, cannabis user and wife of Dim, played by Renaud Rutten.

The actress particularly likes this film but is not convinced by her performance: "[...] I find myself very bad. I make tons, I ham it up, it is unbearable to watch[124].

This wacky Franco-Belgian comedy did not do much better than its predecessors in 2006, with 122,871 tickets sold.

We can also add the film *Fair Play* which recorded 87,832 admissions in France.

> "From his acclaimed short film *(Squash*[125]), the director of *Élodie Bradford*[126], a TV "recurring", makes his first feature film about ordinary violence in the world of executives. Five moments where, around a sport (rowing, golf, rafting...),

124. *Vogue Paris*, #929, August 2012.
125. *Squash*, from 2002, was nominated for a Cesar and an Oscar for best short film.
126. *Élodie Bradford*, French series broadcast between October 2004 and February 2007 on M6, with Arm*Elle* Deutsch in the title role.

work colleagues measure themselves, test themselves and take power. The characters are too emblematic and caricatured, and only Jérémie Renier and Éric Savin get away with it. The ambition of the project turns against it: too clever to be profound. Too bad[127]."

The shooting of *Fair Play*, which started on May 17, 2005 in Prague and ended 41 days later, was not easy for the actors. In addition, a small part of the canyon sequence was shot in France, north of Nice, in the gorges of the Loup and the Clue de la Cerise.

Undoubtedly, these last films will not definitively establish her in the chair of personalities on which French cinema must rely. However, Marion Cotillard saw her career change when she received the script for *La Môme*. If the film was mainly shot in Paris, the cities of Prague and Los Angeles also hosted part of the shooting.

Then, back from Los Angeles, Marion Cotillard illuminates the 59th Cannes Film Festival at the premiere (May 28, 2006) of the film *Transylvania*, by Tony Gatlif. There is already talk of a possible César for the French actress, who is careful not to believe it. But the pages of the monthly magazine *Première*[128] affirm it, really, the promotion ball is well and truly open.

127. Isab*Elle* Danel, *Première*, n° 355, September 2006.
128. *Première*, n° 356, October 2006.

La Môme belongs to him.

During the shooting, Marion - hair shaved on the forehead and shaved eyebrows to perfect the resemblance - did not leave the role. Cut off from her entourage, she could not sleep so much the excitement of the adventure made her nervous. She also suffered in her flesh. From the top of her meter sixty-nine, the actress has tasselled to incarnate the small piece of woman of a meter forty-seven, walking the bent back and the bent knees. It will take intensive sessions of physiotherapy and osteopathy to recover. To play the role of the singer at the end of her days, Marion got up at dawn to undergo up to three, even five hours of make-up. Eight months will be necessary to free her from the influence of Edith Piaf after the shooting of *La Môme*. A role so demanding that she revealed afterwards in an interview with *The Guardian*[129] to have tried several forms of exorcism to get rid of the presence of Edith Piaf.

However, when her interpretation of Piaf was announced, few people believed in her:

> "By the way, when I arrived on the set, I heard
> an extra say, "If Marion Cotillard plays Edith Piaf,
> I'll play Charles de Gaulle."[130]"

129. August 2, 2014 edition.
130. *Studio Magazine*, n° 225, July/August 2006.

The actress was not afraid to accept this role, "but I had moments of dizziness[131]" she says. Marion Cotillard as Piaf will be the performance of the beginning of 2007!

In the meantime, we will find her in Ridley Scott's *A Great Year*, which will symbolize her exceptional 2007 vintage.

With this film made for Fox (Marilyn's studio), Marion Cotillard continues in a secondary role her American career with Russell Crowe, in "headliner". The success is not there, *A Great Year* is not the film that will make her career take off. At least for the moment.

With 166,550 admissions, *Une grande année* also remains a little-known film in France, where it was released on January 3, 2007 - after a Canadian Premiere at the 31st Toronto Film Festival on September 9, 2006.

From Ridley Scott and Russel Crowe - the two men behind the success of *Gladiator*[132] - we expected anything but a romantic comedy. In a world of English financial sharks, Max Skinner, who comes to take possession of the Provençal house bequeathed by his uncle[133], relives his childhood

---

131. *Première*, n° 356, October 2006.
132. *Gladiator*, peplum released in 2000; Russell Crowe received the Oscar for best actor.
133. Uncle Henry, Albert Finney in the film.

memories and remembers that he was once human. The question is: "Will he become one again?" The charm of Fanny, the young owner of the local restaurant, played by Marion Cotillard, leads him to discover the answer.

February 2007: after a first public screening (on the 8th) of *La Môme,* during the opening of the 57th Berlin Film Festival, the Paris Premiere takes place (on the 13th) on the Champs-Élysées in the large hall of the U.G.C. Normandie. This marks a first step for Marion Cotillard: that of the French promotion and, above all, the beginning of a year like no other. "That evening, I felt caught in a whirlwind[134].

A whirlwind that is not about to let her go: the film is released in the wake and, from the first days, it finds its audience. *La Môme sold* 1.6 million tickets in one week. The first figures show that this film will touch several generations. Undeniably, it will remain *the* film of 2007 since it is the biggest success of the year, with more than 5.2 million admissions.

Olivier Dahan and Alain Goldman, CEO of the production company Légende, were never afraid that the subject would be "dated": Piaf[135] is timeless.

----

134. *Studio Magazine*, special edition, December 2007.
135. His disappearance occurred on October 10, 1963 in Grasse but was officially announced on October 11, once his remains were transported clandestinely and illegally to his Parisian apartment on Boulevard Lannes.

Ironically, *La Môme* almost overshadows (the disappointing) *Taxi 4*, which also comes out on February 14. A fourth opus in which the duo Samy Naceri /Frédéric Diefenthal leaves the star to Bernard Farcy, the Commissioner Gibert. Marion Cotillard refused to take part in the film because there was no mention of a fifth installment following this one.

With *La Môme*, she is now critically acclaimed.

> "What can we say about Marion Cotillard? Beyond the mimicry, beyond the gouaille, beyond the impossible positions held by her body, beyond the César awards, her interpretation of Piaf from 20 to 47 years old, until the end of her hands twisted by arthritis, she is so disturbing that she scares the hell out of you. At several points, we lose her. It's as if the life that drives her is not her own. The overused expression "actress possessed" has been laughed at. With her, we bite our tongues[136]."

Behind this flamboyant film are many difficulties: "Three hours of make-up every day... I learned to move like her, to speak like her, to sing like her... The playback was horribly difficult... I was in metaphysical contact with her[137]..."

---

136. Stéphanie Lamome, *Première*, n° 360, February 2007.
137. *Paris Match*, n° 3067, February 28, 2008.

"It may sound abstract, but when I approached a stage, I would just make myself available to welcome Piaf. Sometimes I was even a spectator of what she was doing inside me. It's all quite mystical: Piaf was very attached to Saint Therese. Before each big event, or each concert, she would go and pray in Lisieux or in front of a portrait of Thérèse. I am not a believer, not in the way people think. However, before the shooting, I went to Lisieux and confided in Saint Therese that I was going to need help. I heard this response, whether it came from St. Therese, Piaf, or myself: "You don't need help, you need support." And that's exactly what happened within the team and among the people I was able to meet as we prepared the film. Ginou, Piaf's best friend for twenty years, was particularly supportive. Today, she is my friend[138]."

An almost mystical experience that Marion Cotillard is not likely to forget, just like Ginou Richer, who was very touched by the actress' performance:

"Something strange happened on the set. On the last day, Olivier Dahan had filled the Olympia with extras for the last song of the film: *No, I don't regret it.* I was at the back of the room. Marion came on stage and without realizing it - I swear I don't know how! - when she finished singing, I found myself right next to her. She turned around. We hugged. And there, I said to myself:

---

138. *Première*, n° 353, July 2006.

"She came back! Marion confessed to me that she also felt something very strong at that moment[139]."

"Marion is an exceptional girl. A beautiful soul," says Ginou (Caroline Raynaud in *La Môme*).

With her transcendent interpretation of Edith Piaf in Olivier Dahan's *La Môme*, Marion became "Cotillard", as we say "Adjani", "Deneuve" or "Bardot"... A French star was born, and as such, she joined the Croisette at the 60th Cannes Film Festival, in a rhinestone gown and vintage banana, on the occasion of the Premiere of James Gray's *La nuit nous appartient.*

Behind the scenes, *La Môme was* sold in the United States to American distributor Bob Berney, who didn't hesitate after a few minutes of viewing. "This never happens to me!" he enthused[140].

Renamed *La Vie en rose*[141], Olivier Dahan's film received a *standing ovation* at each of its premieres in New York and Los Angeles. And, just as in France, Marion Cotillard's performance received a rave review from American audiences and critics. "Less a performance than a possession," says *Entertainment Weekly*. "Wonderfully on the mark," exclaims *USA*

139. *Ouest France*, January 16, 2013.
140. *Paris Match*, n° 3067, February 28, 2008.
141. This standard of French song was recorded by Edith Piaf in 1946; *La Vie en rose* gives rhythm to the film *Jeux d'enfants*.

Today. Released on June 10, 2007 in a small number of theaters - this is usual for foreign films - *La Vie en rose* took in $3 million in ten days. At the beginning of July, Marion Cotillard was featured on the cover of *Variety*, a leading professional daily, along with Angelina Jolie and Julie Christie, presenting her as one of the three favorites to be nominated for the Best Actress Oscar.

> "The word 'Oscar' buzzed in my ears pretty quickly, from the first American screening in fact. But it took me a while to realize that it was directly about me. I didn't think that a French actress could be nominated for Best Actress for acting in a French film[142]."

This is forgetting that it happened to Anouk Aimée for *Un homme et une femme* in 1967, Isabelle Adjani for *L'Histoire d'Adèle H.* in 1976, *Camille Claudel* in 1990, Marie-Christine Barrault for *Cousin Cousine* in 1977 as well as to Catherine Deneuve for *Indochine* in 1993. Of course, we do not forget Simone Signoret who obtained it in 1960 but for an English film, *The Paths of the High City*[143]. Sophia Loren is the only actress to have won it for a non-English film with *La Ciociara* in 1962. The Italian

---

142. *Studio Magazine,* special edition, December 2007.
143. Simone Signoret (1921-1985) was nominated again for the Oscar for best actress in 1966 for *La Nef des fous.*

actress did not attend the ceremony, not thinking of being awarded a prize.

At that time, the public hoped that Marion Cotillard would also be rewarded with a Cesar and an Oscar. The result will exceed their expectations. With the Swann d'Or for best actress at the 21st Festival of Romantic Film in Cabourg begins (June 16, 2007) her harvest of awards for her magnificent interpretation of Edith Piaf, the most eternal and international of French singers.

His friend Guillaume Canet was rewarded for his interpretation of a young cook in *Together, that's all*, by Claude Berri. Then both of them will meet (on October [1,] 2007) at the Grand Rex in Paris to be awarded the title of *Frenchie* of the year 2007 at the NRJ Ciné Awards[144]. Since then, the front page of the magazine *Public* released in its exclusive No. 233 of October 27, 2007: "Marion Cotillard, Guillaume Canet: Crazy in love!"

The 100% people news in real time gives birth to a new couple of contemporary cinema in the process of becoming mythical. Yesterday in couple on the screen, today in supposed couple in the city, their love will be made official in London, during the handing-over of the Bafta Awards, on

144. With, in addition, for Marion Cotillard, the NRJ Ciné Award for best "look" for *La Môme*.

February 8, 2008. Marion will let slip in the day a tender gesture for the one who comes to join her and attend her triumphs.

A complicity born five years ago, already when they played Julien and Sophie in *Jeux d'enfants*.

> "For a long time, Guillaume[145] has been the one who reassured me, who found the words to make me less afraid. For example, on Jeunet's film, *Un long dimanche de fiançailles*, I was terrified, convinced that I was not the character, that I would never make it. I called him, he reassured me. And when I started *La Môme*, I was in an indescribable fear. He was also about to start *Ne le dis à personne*[146], an atypical and important project. We will always remember this conversation we both had: we went for a drink together, both of us as anxious as each other about what was ahead of us[147]."

The year 2007 marks the officialization of their relationship. Marion has even left her apartment in the heights of Montmartre for another one, close to Guillaume's house, in the Marais. Like another legendary couple formed by Michèle Morgan and Gérard Oury, they do not live together. She lives in a two-room attic apartment, he lives in a slightly larger duplex. But according to

145. Guillaume Canet and Diane Kruger divorced in January 2006.
146. César 2007 for best director.
147. *Paris Match*, No. 3288, May 24, 2012.

curious observers, we can be sure that no doubt is allowed on their relationship, our two lovebirds are very, very in love.

At 32 years old, Marion Cotillard sees life in pink!

THE OSCAR
- LA MÔME COTILLARD

Since the Swann d'Or, a shower of awards has fallen on Marion Cotillard, including, in addition to the British Bafta, the Golden Globe "Best Actress in a Comedy or Musical", the Prix Lumières and the Golden Star[148]. But Marion Cotillard will live, as an apotheosis, one of the most beautiful weekends of her life. The "Cotillard" made the whole of France fall in love with her, during two of the most prestigious ceremonies.

On Friday, February 22, 2008, at the Théâtre du Châtelet, Marion defeated Isabelle Carré *(Anna M.)*, Cécile de France *(Un secret)*, Marina Foïs *(Darling)* and Catherine Frot *(Odette Toulemonde)* to win the 33rd César for best actress.

After receiving the trophy from the hands of Alain Delon, Marion Cotillard very moved, thanked the director (absent) for having changed her life by writing this beautiful role.

---

148. Ex aequo with Isab*Elle* Carré for *Anna M.*

This continues on Sunday night at the Kodak Theater. "La môme Marion" (as Alain Delon had called her), wins over the American actresses[149]. Marion Cotillard joined in the history of the Oscars Simone Signoret, who had received one 48 years ago[150]. Dressed in a dress designed by Jean-Paul Gaultier and a Chopard diamond necklace, she let her joy explode once again at the 80th Academy Awards ceremony. Forest Whitaker[151] presented her with the supreme award - in the absence of Guillaume Canet, who was following the ceremony in a Los Angeles villa with friends. It is with emotion that she thanks life, love and the world of cinema.

Patrick Bruel, commenting on the ceremony for Canal+, exclaimed, "It's like the victory of Les Bleus in 1998[152]!"

149. She competed with Cate Blanchett *(Elizabeth: The Golden Age)*, Julie Christie *(Far From It)*, Laura Linney *(The Savage Family)* and *Ellen* Page *(Juno)*.
150. Simone Signoret is the first French actress to win the Oscar although this distinction is falsely attributed to Claudette Colbert. Indeed, Claudette Colbert is an actress of French origin, but of American nationality while Simone Signoret is a French actress (of German origin). Other Frenchwomen received the golden statuette for a second role (Lila Kedrova and Juliette Binoche).
151. Forest Whitaker is his partner in Mary by Abel Ferrara and Oscar winner in 2007 for The Last King of Scotland by Kevin Macdonald.
152. "Marion Cotillard, she sees life in pink", *Nous Deux*, n° 3183, July 1st, 2008.

Indeed, for the first time in its history, the Oscars crowned a Frenchwoman in a French role. TF1, as well as foreign producers, were betting more on Juliette Binoche, Vanessa Paradis or Audrey Tautou. Now universally recognized, Marion Cotillard has become one of the emblems of France, crowned on the front page of the national press, including the institutional *Paris Match*[153], while for the Americans, she never ceases to be "the French Siren".

Marion's career is already taking off across the Atlantic. The actress will shoot at the beginning of March *Public Enemies*, with Johnny Depp, then *Nine*, with the Anglo-Irish Daniel Day-Lewis, lucky winner of the 2008 Best Actor Oscar thanks to *There Will Be Blood* by Paul Thomas Anderson. Thus, we can say that she has conquered the American cinema.

"I've always had big dreams," Marion Cotillard told Le *Figaro* on February 25, 2008. Now she is living them. But the new star keeps a cool head: "I have not saved anyone, I have not changed the world. I only played a role[154].

<hr>

153. No. 3067 of February 28, 2008.
154. *Télé 7 jours*, n° 2493, March 8, 2008.

Dior loves it

On February 29, 2008, the Marianne website awkwardly repeated some of Marion Cotillard's comments, collected in the program *Paris Dernière*, rebroadcast on February 26, 2008, on the Paris *Première* channel:

> "I think we are lied to about a lot of things... Coluche, 9/11... Did man really walk on the moon? I've seen a lot of documentaries on that, and that really makes me wonder."

The actress is therefore at the heart of a controversy in France and the United States. Obviously, behind the scenes, Marion Cotillard reacts very badly without retaliating:

> "I wanted to attack immediately because the catchphrase of the article that started it all was totally untrue. But as it risked producing the opposite of the desired effect, I let things die down. Quite quickly in the United States, where the impact was less, less quickly in France. But I was lucky enough to be working

at the time and so be able to concentrate on other things [155]."

Indeed, very quickly, with the shooting of the film *Public Enemies*, directed by Michael Mann [156], the work took over.

> "The day after the Oscars," she says, "I left at 4 a.m. to find myself in the heart of an Indian tribe in Wisconsin... A radical change, to say the least [157]!"

Marion Cotillard plays the role of Evelyn "Billie" Frechette known as Blackbird, the French-Indian fiancée of gangster John Dillinger, played by Johnny Depp.

Needless to say, despite the controversy [158], her future is not threatened either in Hollywood or in France, where she will be again near Guillaume Canet in front of the camera of Karim Dridi. The filming began after the completion of *Public Enemies* and *Nine*. But the controversy in France has obviously hurt her a lot. And while apologizing to

155. *Studio Ciné Live*, n° 1, February 2009.
156. His credits include The Last of the Mohicans, Revelations and Collateral.
157. *Studio Ciné Live*, n° 1, February 2009.
158. In an interview with Globe magazine, Pastor Robert Westman, head of an association of victims of the World Trade Center attacks, asked that the Oscar be withdrawn from Marion Cotillard.

the American people, she still explains herself in the summer issue of *Psychologies magazine*[159]: "That it was very clumsy of me to evoke a subject as serious as September 11 in a television show. This is neither the subject nor the place to do it. And I am far from being the best person to talk about it. But I never claimed, as has been written and said, that it was the insurance companies that destroyed the towers. I just explained that I did not believe everything that the governments and the media were saying. My words have been taken out of context and misrepresented."

Marion Cotillard nevertheless deplores the media "lynching" of which she has been the object (more in France than in the United States).

She concludes, "My only regret is that I hurt people[160]."

Despite her detractors, the "favorite" actress[161] of the French still has the love of the public. At the kick-off of the end-of-year illuminations of the Champs-Élysées (placed under the theme of Europe in 2008), Marion Cotillard inaugurates the event with the mayor of Paris Bertrand Delanoë.

159. No. 276, July-August 2008.
160. *L'Express* n° 3022, June 4, 2009.
161. February 2008: Marion Cotillard is elected in the popularity referendum *Studio Magazine* "favorite female star number 1 of 2007" before Audrey Tautou. On the male side, Guillaume Canet is ranked second behind Louis Garrel *(Les Chansons d'amour)*.

One million white bulbs tinted with a deep blue color adorn the 415 trees of the Champs-Élysées, from the Place de la Concorde to the Arc de Triomphe, since November 19.

"I'm not often in France, so it's true that I'm very happy to be here and it's true that it's a nice thing to illuminate the Champs-Élysées...", she said on the air of R.T.L.

With the city of Paris, she has "[a] very strong bond. Because I was born here, because, culturally, this city is unique. I love it for its museums, for the Place des Vosges, for its cinemas, and especially for the food! I need it and I need France, even if I have hardly been here for more than a year[162]..."

In the eyes of Americans, she embodies the true Parisian, which the actress herself defines as follows: "Perhaps a woman with a certain gouaille? Let's say, a mixture of the populo and the artistic. I come from an artistic background and I have always attached importance to culture. In this, I am very French, and very Parisian[163]."

That's not all: she was chosen by John Galliano to become the muse for the next Lady Dior, the mythical bag of the luxury brand - created, according to the "legend" for the visit to France in

162. *L'Express* n° 3022, June 4, 2009.
163. *Ibid.*

September 1995 of Lady Di (on an initiative of Bernadette Chirac).

> "The adventure with Dior was motivated by my admiration for John Galliano, who is a genius, for the prestige of the house and because it was a very cinematic project broadcast on the Internet. There are no TV spots[164]."

Peter Lindbergh will be responsible for the first advertising campaign for the spring-summer 2009 collection. At the same time, it will be accompanied by a promotional short film of 6 minutes 30, entitled *The Lady Noire Affair*, directed by Olivier Dahan for Dior. This one will lead Marion Cotillard in a dark atmosphere, from the streets of Paris to the top of the Eiffel Tower.

On May 21, 2009, as part of the 62nd Cannes Film Festival, Marion Cotillard, sublime in Dior with Chopard jewels, appeared on the arm of Guillaume Canet, for the amfAR evening under the presidency of Sharon Stone. This event is intended to raise funds for the fight against AIDS, the very chic Eden Roc, known as the Hotel du Cap, a legendary establishment located in Cap d'Antibes.

It is clear that the ultraglamorous couple is highly anticipated for their on-screen reunion in what

---

164. *L'Express* n° 3022, June 4, 2009.

promises to be a great romantic adventure film. It is an adaptation of the novel by Sylvain Estibal, *The Last Flight of Lancaster*, published in 2003. The shooting, which began on March 9, was completed in Merzouga, Morocco, after eight weeks of work. The release in theaters is scheduled for November 18, 2009.

Glorious run with Johnny Depp

Public Enemies was released in French theaters on July 8, 2009, after an international premiere on June 18 in Chicago, where it was partly shot. This feature film recounts the hunt for John Dillinger, a bank robber who marked the era of the Great Depression, by the F.B.I. The famous criminal - considered as "Robin Hood" or as "Public Enemy No. 1" by the F.B.I. boss, J. Edgar Hoover (Billy Crudup) - was shot at the age of 31, in July 1934. He had just come out of a Chicago movie theater, after seeing the film *Public Enemy No. 1* (with Clark Gable in the title role, but also Myrna Loy, of whom Dillinger was a great admirer). Marion Cotillard became an accomplice and companion of Dillinger on screen for a secondary role, under the direction of director Michael Mann, whom she admires a lot: "Michael Mann's investment is fascinating. He does not let go... We redo the take until it suits him[165]."

Michael Mann thinks no less of her:

---

165. *Studio Ciné Live* n° 1, February 2009.

> "Watching her play in *La Môme*, you can feel a remarkable authenticity in each of her gestures. She transcends herself to be the character. Her artistic and intellectual commitment is total. I remember that the boss of Universal was convinced that she would not be able to get rid of her French accent. And yet she did. She worked hard to do it. That's what makes the difference in this business[166]."

Despite a commendable investment, Marion Cotillard was very stressed about not having a Midwestern accent to the point that this obsession triggered physical reactions in her: "I had to leave at 4 a.m. in a disaster for a hospital in Chicago after doubling in volume[167] !" It was therefore impossible for Marion to feel relaxed during the shooting and to feel a total pleasure to shoot with Johnny Depp and Michael Mann.

> "The shots were multiplying, it was driving poor Johnny Depp crazy. It took Michael Mann himself to ask me to stop being afraid, reassuring me about the French origins of my character[168]..."

1.5 million French viewers rushed to see this lesson in history and cinema, delivered with elegance and great efficiency by Michael Mann.

---

166. *Studio Ciné Live* n° 6, summer 2009.
167. *Studio Ciné Live* n° 1, February 2009.
168. *Télérama* n° 3252, May 12, 2012.

And, if we look closely, Marion Cotillard is not simply, to use a very common expression in the United States, the *love interest* of the hero. Indeed "Marion Cotillard devours the screen with her talent to convey in a glance, in a gesture all the feelings of the world[169]."

Marion Cotillard continues her Hollywood career by joining the cast of the film *Inception*, "a science fiction and action film that explores the twists and turns of the mind", starring the great Leonardo DiCaprio. She will therefore leave, on October 8, 2009, Cap-Ferret and the shooting of The *Little Handkerchiefs* (which began on August 6) to join (in Los Angeles, in the Warner studios) the director Christopher Nolan and the team of *Inception* on October 10. The shooting will start on June 19, 2009 in Tokyo to continue in Great Britain and Paris: the film is already one of the most anticipated of the year 2010.

Cap-Ferret - although nicknamed the "Saint-Tropez of the Atlantic" in the summer - is a seaside resort sought after for its calm and, of course, for the beauty of the Arcachon basin.

> "It is one of the most beautiful places in the world! I fell in love with this place where I just shot Guillaume Canet's *Les Petits Mouchoirs*.

169. Thierry Chèze, *Studio Ciné Live*, n° 6, summer 2009.

> Everything is beautiful and preserved. Even though I discovered it a short time ago, I feel like it's a part of me[170]."

Cap-Ferret is also a place that the director Guillaume Canet knows very well. That's why he chose to shoot his third film there, for which he wrote the script alone for the first time.

> "I wrote the script after a vacation with friends, in a barrack, where I realized that we could spend two weeks with friends without really talking to each other. It was only necessary to have fun, and especially not to show that we are not doing well[171]."

For this story, Guillaume Canet composed a cast with actors close to him, who have an emotional bond with him or with each other. The result is a cast of equal importance: François Cluzet, Valérie Bonneton, Benoît Magimel, Gilles Lellouche, Jean Dujardin (in a slightly less important role), the comedian Laurent Lafitte (whose character of Antoine was to be played by Guillaume Canet at the beginning), Pascale Arbillot, Anne Marivin and of course Marion Cotillard (as well as her parents, Niseema Theillaud and Jean-Claude Cotillard).

170. *Studio Ciné Live* n° 10, December 2009.
171. *Studio Ciné Live* n° 20, November 2010.

As surprising as it is, Marion Cotillard claims, since her awards, to receive fewer scripts than before[172]!

The Last Flight is released in France on December 16, 2009: in the French Sahara in 1933. Bill Lancaster, a famous English pilot, has disappeared during an attempt to set a record for a crossing between London and Cape Town. His mistress, the adventurer and aviatrix Marie Vallières de Beaumont[173] (Marion Cotillard) has only one obsession, to find him. While flying over the Ténéré, the young woman is forced to land her biplane near an advanced post of French meharists. Captain Vincent Brosseau (Guillaume Marquet) welcomes her, but refuses to help her.

This romantic film produced by Gaumont with a budget of 12.3 million euros stars the couple Marion Cotillard / Guillaume Canet, who are present to discuss the film in the press. They were interviewed together on the France 2 news on the Sunday before the release, by the host Laurent Delahousse. But nothing happens and the cinematographic reunion of the couple Cotillard-Canet disappoints. The critics are mixed. Some see it as

172. *Studio Ciné Live* n° 1, February 2009.
173. Marie Vallières de Beaumont in the film is actually the aviatrix Chubbie Miller who had made a promise to herself and Bill Lancaster, with whom she had a passionate affair, that if one of them crashed, the other would come and get him.

an *English Patient*[174] à la française, others reproach the film for its slowness. Here is an example:

> "The only thing left is a scenario that goes haywire in the second part of the story where the couple gets lost in the middle of the desert, multiplying ellipses until... more thirsty[175]."

In theaters, the start was disappointing with 147,000 admissions in the first week. In the second week, the drop is moderate. *The Last Flight* only reached 363,084 admissions.

It was a great disappointment for the actress, whose return to the French cameras since *La Môme*[176], after two shoots in the United States (*Public Enemies* and *Nine*). On December 15, 2009 came the announcement of her nomination for the Golden Globe "Best Actress in a Comedy or *Musical*[177]" for *Nine*. Marion Cotillard cannot, despite her international aura and her popularity with the press (and women's magazines in particular) be the sole guarantor of a cinematic success.

174. Film by Anthony Minghella with Ralph Fiennes and Kristin Scott Thomas, awarded nine Oscars in 1997.
175. Fabrice Leclerc, *Studio Ciné Live* n° 11, January 2010.
176. At the end of August 2006, she was to shoot in the south of France with Gilles Lellouche, *Le Mauvais Œil*, a thriller that was to be the first film of Félicie Dutertre and François Rabes.
177. The winner is Meryl Streep, for the film Julia and Julia by Nora Ephron.

Marion, who was involved in the adventure before Guillaume, says: "I remember that at the time, when I talked to him about the film, he shared my enthusiasm. He was very moved by this story... Soon enough, it became obvious for us to make this film together[178]." It is therefore a real disappointment for the one who fought for the project and for the director Karim Dridi *(Pigalle, Bye-Bye)*. "And then I spent two months in the middle of the desert wanting to kill him and resenting myself for having agreed to defend him when he was very bad[179]", she will admit afterwards. Words that could only make the French-Tunisian director Karim Dridi react:

> "Why didn't Marion Cotillard say what was on her mind when the film was released in 2009? When I hear her say today that she can't be good when she doesn't like the director, I am flabbergasted. If she's not a pro, then let her give back the $1 million check for the eight weeks of shooting she was given[180]."

Marion Cotillard was nominated in the category of female despair at the 5th ceremony of the Gérard du cinéma, distinguishing each year the "worst" French productions of the previous year.

------

178. cinemotions.com, press kit of the film The Last Flight.
179. *Closer*.fr, 22 November 2012.
180. *Sud Ouest*, January 27, 2013.

"I really wanted to have it[181]!" quipped Marion. "Without wanting to be mean, I already had my thank you speech: 'Without this director, none of this would have been possible.'" However, it was Virginie Efira who won the cinder block, this May 10, 2010, for her role in *The Whistler* by (and with) Philippe Lefebvre.

For Marion Cotillard, this experience has allowed her to live magical moments, especially thanks to her camera: "Thanks to it, I recently lived magical moments in Morocco, on the set of The *Last Flight*. We met Berber tribes, with children that I photographed and could give them the images instantly. It was very powerful[182]."

The Last Flight was - without any impact on the careers of the two actors - an artistic and industrial disaster.

181. *Closer*.fr, 22 November 2012.
182. *Studio Ciné Live*, n° 20, November 2010.

INCEPTION AND *THE LITTLE HANDKERCHIEFS*

On February 27, 2010, at the age of 34, she is the president of the 35th César ceremony, which takes place at the Théâtre du Châtelet.

With nine Césars, Jacques Audiard's *Un prophète* reigned supreme at this year's event, which was marked by two records: a fifth statuette for Isabelle Adjani *(La Journée de la jupe)* and a Best Newcomer/ Best Actor double for Tahar Rahim *(Un prophète)*.

At the end of this night of the César Awards, our glamorous icon in a Dior dress looks back on the role that was entrusted to her:

> "It's an exercise I'm not used to doing. I'm not necessarily comfortable doing it, but it was nice to do it[183]."

On March 15, 2010, a new distinction was added to Marion Cotillard's list of achievements. Indeed, on that Monday, Frédéric Mitterrand, Minister of Culture, elevated her to the honorary

183. premiere.fr, February 28, 2010.

rank of Knight of the Order of Arts and Letters, at the Ministry of Culture, along with filmmaker Tim Burton, who receives the insignia of officer.

Frédéric Mitterrand praised Marion's "obvious charm, natural grace and beauty", emphasizing that these "things" cannot be learned. "It is a magical gift, but one must know how to receive and carry it. She is "this movement that moves the lines" of which Baudelaire speaks," he continues. Before concluding his speech with these words:

> "I am well aware that I am paying tribute today to an artist *in progress*, as is also Tim Burton - I do not mean of course "in progress", but in movement, in full bloom, because your Oscar was not only a culmination, a consecration, but above all the starting point of an immense career that has not ceased to dazzle us, to enchant us and especially to move us[184]."

For the anecdote, if Marion Cotillard had a start during this ceremony, it is because Frédéric Mitterrand, surely carried away by the emotion, unfortunatly pushes the tip of the decoration in her skin, piercing her blouse, the actress almost falling from the top of her stilettos.

---

184. culturecommunication.gouv.fr

Things finally went back to normal, and "the Cotillard" was able to thank the French Republic for this honor.

Marion, moved and elegant, was accompanied by Guillaume Canet.

Nine, released in December 2009 in the United States, will be released in France on March 3, 2010. It is a musical that pays homage to Federico Fellini's *Eight and a Half*[185], telling us the story of an Italian film maestro who is out of inspiration, trying to escape from his new film.

From the trailer, we are promised a *musical*: "dazzling, visionary, electric", according to the American bi-monthly *Rolling Stone*, or "[s]pectacular, glamorous and sexy", for the French film magazine *Première*. However, despite its prestigious cast of Marion Cotillard (Luisa, the wife), Nicole Kidman (Claudia, the star), Penélope Cruz (Carla, the mistress), Sophia Loren (La mamma), Kate Hudson and Fergie[186] surrounding Daniel Day-Lewis (Guido, the maestro in question) and with an ace musical director, Rob Marshall *(Chicago)* at the helm of the film, *Nine did* not seduce the crowds

---

185. Released in 1963, with Marcello Mastroianni (Guido), Claudia Cardinale (Claudia, the star), Anouk Aimée (Luisa, the wife), Sandra Milo (Carla, the mistress) and Giuditta Risson (La mamma).
186. Stacy Ann Ferguson aka Fergie, American singer, figurehead of the Black Eyed Peas, is also an actress.

across the Atlantic or in France. The $20 million capitalized did not make up for the $80 million invested. Thus, the film did not meet the expectations of the producers, who had to be satisfied with little, also in France, with nearly 360,000 entries.

Consequently, Marion Cotillard - who came to present the film on the set of the *Grand Journal,* opposite Michel Denisot, on February 18, 2010, alongside Penélope Cruz and Daniel Day-Lewis - is disappointed and says she is "quite sad that people did not get hooked on it." "Maybe people were expecting something more commercial[187]," she also says.

Still, this film remains an incredible experience. "An absolute dream! When I was little, my dream was to become an actress and to be able to play in a musical one day[188]." However, three weeks after having finished *Public Enemies*, she arrives exhausted on the set. Marion had trouble getting to rehearsals and gradually lost her enthusiasm.

> "Every morning I think, 'Are you crazy? How many girls dream of being in your shoes? How can you go there backwards?" But my body just doesn't keep up! And then, in three days of rehearsals, I run into Nicole Kidman, Penélope Cruz, Kate Hudson, Fergie, Judie Dench, Sophia Loren

187. non-stop-people.com, January 6, 2015.
188. *Studio Magazine*, n° Hors série, December 2007.

and Daniel Day-Lewis. I realize that we will all be in the same studio for two months. And I understand that we all have the same fears about the necessary technique. Suddenly, fatigue gave way to euphoria, which never left me[189]."

Today, the young actress loves the film. "And I know that Rob Marshall loves the film too and is very proud of it[190]" she says.

Therefore, the posterity of the film is assured, and his performance was awarded on January 5, 2010 with the Desert Palm Achievement Award at the 21st edition of the International Film Festival in Palm Springs, California. One of the songs from the soundtrack *(Take It All) is on* the list of nominations for the Academy Award for Best Song[191] and, finally, his performance was praised by Rob Marshall himself:

"I knew Marion through *La Môme*. Her composition was extraordinary but I did not know the extent of her palette. So I auditioned her for several roles. First, logically, that of the costume designer since she had to sing *Folies Bergère*. Then, I asked her to interpret *Unusual Way*, the song of Claudia, Guido's icon and muse, a perfect role for her who

189. *Studio Ciné Live*, n° 1, February 2009.
190. non-stop-people.com, January 6, 2015.
191. Winner *The Weary Kind*, played by Colin Farrell in Crazy Heart, by Scott Cooper.

has the mystery of the Claudia Cardinale of the time. And I wanted to hear her in *My Husband Makes Movie*. There, her interpretation blew me away. I saw Guido's wife in front of me and the whole film through her eyes[192]."

Her charm dazzled at the 63rd Cannes Film Festival, which took place from May 12 to 23, 2010, under the presidency of Tim Burton.

French star of international renown and muse of the Dior house, Marion Cotillard is becoming a regular on the Croisette.

"You get to meet people you don't often get to meet, it's a really nice place[193]."

On the program: the Chopard evening, May 18, at the VIP Room, for which she opted for a *glam-rock* look in a glittering suit, signed Lefranc-Ferrant. She also accompanied Guillaume Canet to Cannes, where he unveiled a preview of two minutes of his next film, *Les Petits Mouchoirs*, on May 17 at Michel Denisot's *Grand Journal*.

Marion Cotillard is about to join Woody Allen's next film, *Midnight in Paris*, which begins shooting in the City of Light in July 2010. This film projects her in the 1920s alongside Owen Wilson (for a

192. *Studio Ciné Live*, n° 13, March 2010.
193. premiere.fr, 18 May 2010.

role that Woody Allen would have played without hesitation had he been younger[194]). Fourteen years after his musical film *Tout le monde dit I Love You*, it is finally the return to the French capital of the very urban director for whom Paris is a dream city. Then in the fall, Marion Cotillard will face a deadly virus in Steven Soderbergh, alongside his favorite actress, Kate Winslet.

> "I've seen almost all of her films and she's someone who inspires me, who I can relate to. I love her choices, the way she embraces roles, the woman she is, her simplicity, her involvement. I like everything about her! I find her sublime. I feel that she is not afraid of anything in her characters, that she always goes all the way... And one of the most beautiful moments of my life as an actress, outside of filming, was to give her an Oscar[195]. It was even more incredible than receiving it myself. It was an immense happiness to be on stage talking about her, when, since *Heavenly Creatures*[196], I have fallen in love with this girl[197]."

194. Woody Allen was born on December 1st, 1935, making him 74 years old.

195. On February 22, 2009, Kate Winslet received the Oscar for best actress for the film *The Reader* by Stephen Daldry. She is also (and above all) the heroine of James Cameron's film Titanic, released in France in January 1998.

196. The film *Heavenly Creatures*, by Peter Jackson, was released in France in July 1996.

197. *Studio Ciné Live*, n° 10, December 2009.

But her greatest encounter was definitely with Meryl Streep. The fact that the most nominated actress in the history of the Oscars knows her and appreciates her work overwhelmed her: "She is the ultimate actress: unstoppable and authentic[198]."

For the time being, *Inception will* be released in France on July 21, 2010, after a world premiere in London on July 8. For his sixth feature film, Christopher Nolan delivers both a spy movie and a science fiction film that is almost impossible to summarize: "*Inception* is not a movie whose story is told because everyone will have a different interpretation of it[199]."

Marion is truly transported by this experience:

> "Despite the moments of panic that it can cause me, I love nothing more than to be taken on board by someone located in a universe far from mine[200]."

The *Inception* of the title is the powerful power to "extract" dreams - and therefore secrets - that Cobb (Leonardo DiCaprio) and his team have. This is the first time the director of *Memento* (2000) has made a choral film. *Inception is* based on a group of very different actors and characters. For him, this was a major project with a budget of 160

198. *Madame Figaro*, n° 20396, February 27, 2010.
199. *Studio Ciné Live*, n° 17, July 2010.
200. *Studio Ciné Live*, n° 17, July 2010.

million dollars, with a five-month shoot that took place in six different countries. After Japan, the team headed to Great Britain before making stops in Paris, Morocco, Los Angeles and finally Calgary, in the middle of the Canadian mountains.

For Christopher Nolan,

> "Leonardo was the first to join the project. Marion plays his wife in the film. She plays an essential role in the plot of *Inception*. What I like about Marion is that she is a terrible femme fatale, like the great Hollywood stars of the golden age of silent films. She is mysterious, she has this incredible grace, she creates a timeless image of the woman[201]."

For Leonardo DiCaprio: "Marion has indeed this typically Hollywood glamour. But above all, she's an actress who takes on her character in every detail. I have known her for a long time, even before *La Môme*, since Guillaume Canet is one of my best friends[202]. And I've always known her like that: she gives everything she has. That's rare[203]."

On the downside, Marion Cotillard's detractors can nevertheless rejoice in her nomination for the

---

201. *Studio Ciné Live*, n° 17, July 2010.
202. Since Danny Boyle's film *The Beach*, shot on an island southeast of Bangkok, in early 1999.
203. *Studio Ciné Live*, n° 17, July 2010.

Gérard du désespoir féminin 2011[204] for her interpretation of Mall in *Inception* at the 6th - and penultimate - edition of the satirical awards.

Inception was a worldwide success during the summer of 2010. In France, this *blockbuster* was hailed by critics and awarded four technical Oscars[205]. It came in third place with nearly 5 million tickets sold, behind *The Little Handkerchiefs* with 5.5 million, and finally number 1 *Harry Potter and the Deathly Hallows - Part 1*, by David Yates with 6 million tickets sold.

Finally, *Inception is* described by *Le Journal du Dimanche* as "a slap in the face like we see every 10 years at the cinema[206]."

October 20, 2010 marks the public release of the film *Les Petits Mouchoirs*. In this work, friends meet for a summer that will reveal them to themselves and Guillaume Canet talks about him, about us and about all these little lies that eat away at our lives. "It's true that the film is a rather harsh statement on friendship, or rather on the group[207]"

---

204. Gérard won on February 21, 2011 by Jane Birkin for *Thelma, Louise and Chantal,* who was also in competition with Isab*Elle* Adjani *(Mammuth)*, Carole Bouquet *(Libre échange)*, Mathilde Seigner (Camping 2) and Audrey Tautou *(De vrais mensonges)*.
205. Best photography, best sound, best sound editing and best visual effects.
206. *Le Journal du Dimanche,* July 17, 2010.
207. *Studio Ciné Live*, n° 20, November 2010.

confides Guillaume Canet who recognizes an auto-biographical part behind his characters.

> "In Max, played by François Cluzet, I find my ability to get angry at the drop of a hat and the way I was able to lock myself into work, even on vacation. Through Antoine [Laurent Lafitte], I evoke my period as a man-child when I asked everyone's opinion. Éric [Gilles Lellouche] embodies the need to seduce at all costs, which I felt at one point in my life. Marie, played by Marion Cotillard, reflects the time when I didn't want to commit myself. I was unable to fall asleep next to a one-night stand[208]!"

Directing his partner might seem difficult, but according to Guillaume Canet it is "[t]ruly easy, on the contrary, because she is very talented, concentrated and hard-working. But I didn't want to consider her as anything other than a character in the group. So I was a little more sparing with compliments than I was with the others! I didn't want to privilege her, which must have been complicated for her. Living with the director is not easy because in the evening, he brings up all the problems of the day and the next day[209]".

For Marion Cotillard, playing under the direction of her partner :

208. lefigaro.fr, 19 October 2010.
209. lefigaro.fr, 19 October 2010.

"It's great! Behind the camera, Guillaume is very perfectionist, but he empathizes with his actors. I've worked with directors who had such a hard time expressing what they wanted and guiding me in the play, that I would have preferred they didn't tell me. Guillaume has a gift for finding the right words to connect you to your character. I have rarely had such an easy time reaching such emotions in the movies! He never gave me more attention than the others. This is a choral film, there is no leading man: to play the game, you had to be part of the gang[210]."

The critics were very divided for the film as well as for the actors: "Cotillard, undisputed *recordwoman* of whining, achieves a new feat by adding to the traditional tears the little gesture that belongs only to the great champions: the dripping *(sic) of* the nose[211]."

Only Valérie Bonneton and Gilles Lellouche win the prize by receiving a nomination for the César for Best Supporting Actress[212] and for Best Supporting Actor[213]. On the other hand, François

<hr>

210. lexpress.fr, October 19, 2010.
211. Jean-Baptiste MORAIN, lesinrock.com, 19 October 2010 [online]. URL: <http://www.lesinrocks.com/cinema/films-a-l-affiche/les-petits-mouchoirs/>. Accessed September 14, 2016.
212. Winner: Anne Alvaro for *Le Bruit des glaçons* by Bertrand Blier.
213. Winner: Michael Lonsdale for *Des hommes et des dieux*, by Xavier Beauvois.

Cluzet[214] "wins" the Brutus[215] for Best Actor, an award for the worst of the French film industry, like the Gérard du Cinéma. The weekly magazine for film and audiovisual professionals, *Le Film français, awarded* Guillaume Canet, on February 3, 2011, at the Palais de Tokyo, the French Film Trophy[216]. *The Little Handkerchiefs won* first place among the French films of the year 2010. The public recognized itself in this band of friends. A generational comedy is born!

For the general public, it is during this period that Marion Cotillard reveals herself as a singer, especially during the program *Vivement dimanche*, scheduled on October 10, 2010 with, as guest of the day, Guillaume Canet in full promotion of The *Little Handkerchiefs*. That day, she appeared to sing *Five Thousand Nights*, a duet with Yodelice and *More Than Meets The Eye as a* backup singer. She also joined the group on the set of *Taratata*, the following November 2, to sing together *Velvet Goldmine* by David Bowie and, still as a backup singer, for the title *More Than Meets The Eye* by Yodelice.

----

214. François Cluzet and Valerie Bonneton, a couple in the city as well as on screen for years, separated a few days after the release of the film *The Little Handkerchiefs*.
215. Where, last year, Marion Cotillard was nominated best actress for *The Last Flight* (winner: Isab*Elle* Adjani for *The Day of the Skirt* by Jean-Paul Lilienfeld).
216. *La Môme* received the same award in 2007.

Maxim Nucci, singer and *leader* of the group Yodelice, is no stranger to Marion Cotillard or Guillaume Canet, since he is also in The *Little Handkerchiefs*. He plays Franck, the character who assumes his feelings and finally gives Marie the strength to believe in their story. This fiercely independent globetrotter, whose lovers are asked to leave as soon as their work is done, is played by Marion Cotillard. A character of a woman of today, for whom it is impossible for her to disappear behind a costume and a hairstyle of the time, a language.

> "When I get there, I see things on the screen that I feel are mine, just mine, and it's unbearable. Probably because I don't find myself interesting enough[217]."

With Yodelice, Marion Cotillard multiplies her musical adventures. She has always loved to sing.

Let's also note his interpretations (*live)* of *Milord* (in duet with Jenifer[218]) and *Les Amants d'un jour* in a show[219] tribute to Edith Piaf in 2007.

> "I've always dreamed of being in a band and Maxim, a friend of mine for ten years, gave me

217. *Télérama*, No. 3252, May 12, 2012.
218. At the time, the singer Jenifer was in couple with Maxim Nucci.
219. "La Môme Piaf", on TF1, February 10, 2007.

the wonderful gift of inviting me to join his band. At first, he called me to do backing vocals on his new album[220], but we ended up doing a duet[221]. Then he asked me to participate in his tour: so that no one would recognize me, I went on stage wearing a hat and a man's suit, under the pseudonym of Simone, the first name of my grandmother - maternal - who dreamed of a career as a singer[222]!"

Without knowing if she was joking or not, Marion heard her say: "I would have liked to be a singer, but there was already the kid Piaf[223]!"

Bassist, percussionist, pianist and singer on May 15, 2010 on the stage of the Olympia, then in November at the Bataclan and at the Cigale: the talents that the actress, now recognized, are therefore numerous. Marion Cotillard defines herself as "[p]ersevering, passionate and curious[224]". And among her musical encounters, there was Madonna, in 2008!

"When I was 12 years old, I was a total fan of hers and I had attended her show at the Parc de

220. Cardioid, in stores on October 25th 2010.
221. Five Thousand Nights.
222. lexpress.fr, October 19, 2010.
223. *Madame Figaro*, n° 1166, December 30, 2006.
224. *Paris Match*, n° 3170, February 18, 2010.

Sceaux[225]. Now she was in London[226] and, after her concert, I had the chance to talk to her. I knew that she had said many beautiful things about *La Môme*. This moment will remain mythical. All the more so as it was she who came to me after her concert. Imagine the scene! I will never forget it[227]."

In 2008, the Queen of Pop was full of praise for the young Frenchwoman:

"I found Marion Cotillard striking in *La Môme*. To the point of jealousy. I would have loved to direct this film and to have directed her[228]."

225. On August 29, 1987, Madonna performed in front of 130,000 spectators at the Parc de Sceaux (92) as part of her first *Who's That Girl* Tour.
226. On September 11, 2008 at Wembley Stadium, as part of his *Sticky and Sweet* Tour.
227. *Studio Ciné Live*, n° 1, February 2009.
228. *Studio Magazine*, n° 249, September 2008.

The birth of Marcel and the shooting with Woody Allen

Here we are in 2011. Marion Cotillard is pregnant. It is the American website people.com that announced the news, which will be made official by Marion Cotillard's representative in Los Angeles to the A.F.-P. and the American media. The French *management* team has also confirmed the pregnancy, which made the front page of *Paris Match* No. 3217 of January 13, 2011. The birth is then expected for the spring. Therefore, it will be impossible for her to go to the shooting of David Cronenberg's *Cosmopolis*, which is scheduled to begin on May 23, 2011 in Manhattan before continuing in Toronto, Canada, the director's native country. The main character of the film will be played by Robert Pattinson, after Colin Farrell has also withdrawn from the project. It is finally the Canadian actress Sarah Gadon who will replace Marion Cotillard as Robert Pattinson's devoted wife for the film.

As good news never comes alone, for the first time in nine years, the highest paid actor in the 7th art is an actress! And that with 2.35 million euros of income for Marion Cotillard. She is just ahead of Jean Dujardin (2.3 million euros), Kad Merad (2.25 million euros), Romain Duris (2.04 million euros) and Gérard Depardieu (2 million euros), according to the list established (February 21, 2011) by *Le Figaro*.

Last July, in Paris, during a press conference to promote the film *Inception*, Leonardo DiCaprio called it a "national treasure".[229]

Money has never counted in Marion Cotillard's artistic choices: she even accepted a more modest remuneration when she went from *Taxi* to *Taxi 2*.

> "I'm completely out of touch with the money. When I'm offered peanuts, I realize it - I'm not stupid - but I'll never fight for millions of dollars. It's not in my nature[230]."

"Marion Cotillard gave birth yesterday - Thursday, May 19, 2011 - in Paris[231]. It is a little boy and his name is Marcel. Everything went well," said the agency Adéquat[232] to the A.F.-P.

This is the role of a lifetime that begins for Marion Cotillard (35) and Guillaume Canet (38).

---

229. lefigaro.fr, July 9, 2010.
230. *Première*, n° 356, October 2006.
231. At the American Hospital of Paris, in Neuilly-sur-Seine (92).
232. Art agency representing Marion Cotillard.

Unfortunately, Léontine, her beloved grandmother, did not see the child: she passed away last February, at almost 102 years old. On several occasions in the media, Marion Cotillard spoke of all the love she has for the mother of her father. In fact, one of the happiest days of her life - on April 2, 2007 - was when she organized a screening of *La Môme* at the cinema Le Cithéa, in Plouguenast, for her Breton grandmother and the co-residents of her retirement home. Marion Cotillard frequently visited her at the retirement home Les Quatre Couleurs in Loudéac, not far from Plémet in the Côtes-d'Armor - where Léontine had settled with her husband, Édouard Cotillard, for their retirement (after having worked as a cleaning lady and he as a market gardener, then as a municipal employee in Alfortville); he died in April 2000. The actress had then confided:

> "I try to come as often as possible, for my grandmother's birthday, her anniversary: I always get emotional when I find her[233]..."

Because of the imminent birth of the little Marcel, Marion Cotillard could not go up the steps of Cannes on May 11, 2011 for the last film of Woody Allen *Midnight in Paris*, which was the opening (out of competition) of the 64th Festival, chaired by Robert De Niro.

233. *Ouest France*, February 26, 2008.

However, he did not lack the desire to do so:

> "It was the first time I had the opportunity to walk up the steps for a film in the selection[234], and a film by Woody Allen moreover[235]."

On the red carpet, the team of the film was indeed represented by Woody Allen himself, surrounded by Adrien Brody, Léa Seydoux, Owen Wilson, Rachel McAdams and Michael Sheen but without Marion Cotillard or Carla Bruni!

For Marion Cotillard, "[t]his film was [...] an experience as exciting as it was destabilizing. Woody Allen sent me the script and we talked about it by phone, but I only met him four days before the shooting! So, at first, I was petrified. I had seen all his films, read all his books: I wanted so much to please him, to live up to his expectations, that I put terrible pressure on myself[236].

The actress is full of praise for the New Yorker:

> "He has the power to transform actresses, to make them "Woodyallenian": he chose my clothes - often male costumes - my make-up, my hairstyles, made me change my look, my accent... And

---

234. With the exception of *Comment je me suis disputé... (ma vie sexuElle)* by Arnaud Desplechin in 1996, in which we only get a glimpse of her.
235. *Madame Figaro*, n° 20765, May 7, 2011.
236. lexpress.fr, May 10, 2011.

he made me howl with laughter! Only he could invent sentences like: "I would like to end on a message of hope. I don't have one. In exchange, would two messages of despair suit you[237]"?"

According to Woody Allen, Marion Cotillard is a "great actress, who puts life into the dialogue. Her acting is very natural, her face so expressive. She does not play, she is. With the many actresses he has directed throughout his impressive filmography, one can say that he knows what he is talking about. He adds:

"I worked with two great actresses before her: Maureen Stapleton and Geraldine Page[238]. Maureen was one of those actresses who knew her lines inside out and wouldn't leave them even if a plane flew overhead at the time of the take. With Geraldine, the plane would have been part of the scene. Marion is like Geraldine Page[239]."

This romantic comedy - whose poster is partly based on Vincent Van Gogh's *Starry Night* (1889) - tells the story of the Parisian adventures of Gil Pender (Owen Wilson), a writer in need of inspiration, who is invited at the stroke of midnight to get into an old car that takes him to the artistic Paris of

237. lexpress.fr, October 19, 2010.
238. Maureen Stapleton and Geraldine Page were his interpreters in the film *Interiors*, released in 1978.
239. *Le Journal du Dimanche*, May 8, 2011.

the 1920s, to meet Adriana, who is then the muse of avant-garde painters - Adriana being played by Marion Cotillard, who is more luminous than ever.

This new film by the indefatigable Woody Allen, the eleventh to be screened at Cannes since *Manhattan* (1979), is rather well received. It is a pleasant surprise for festival-goers in general and critics in particular, including Pierre Murat. "In an airy and playful tone, Woody Allen finds his favorite subject: the eternal dissatisfaction of the living," he writes for *Télérama*[240] "And it looks like happiness," he continues.

With 1.7 million admissions, *Midnight in Paris was* a great success in France, one of the most important for the filmmaker with *The Purple Rose of Cairo* (1985), *Vicky Cristina Barcelona* (2008) and *Manhattan* (1979).

In 2012, Woody Allen was awarded the Oscar for Best Original Screenplay, failing to win the Oscar for Best Picture and Best Director. This one was awarded to the French film *The Artist* and Michel Hazanavicius - and with him Jean Dujardin, awarded best actor for his portrayal of George Valentin, fallen star of silent cinema.

---

240. *Télérama*, n° 3200, May 14, 2011.

Greenpeace

While she has just given birth to her first child, Marion Cotillard continues to be solicited by filmmakers, mostly American. Thus, in early June 2011, we learn that James Gray has just hired her for his next film, entitled *The Immigrant*, alongside Joaquin Phoenix and Jeremy Renner. The shooting was then to take place only the following year, given the busy schedule of Marion Cotillard who was then starting the shooting of the last part of the *Batman* trilogy. Christopher Nolan, who had already directed her in *Inception*, wants to work with her again by giving her the role of Miranda Tate, the great villain of the most anticipated *blockbuster of* 2012: *The Dark Knight Rises*. It is rather a small role.

One wonders if his choices are determined by the names of the directors or by the roles they offer him:

> "On the combination of the two. But I still have to be moved by the script first. And usually, if I'm not sure I can play a character, I go for it. It's exciting to think that maybe you're not the right person, that you'll never get it right, and then

eventually find an authenticity and, therefore, enjoyment in acting[241]."

But now, one of his dreams is gone: the director Claude Chabrol[242] passed away on September 12, 2010, at the age of 80. "I always dreamed of shooting with Claude Chabrol, my idol of French cinema, now it will not happen. It was one of my greatest dreams as an actress, as great as the one to shoot with Woody Allen[243]."

On the other hand, Jacques Audiard, strengthened by the success of *A Prophet* (Grand Prix of the 62nd Cannes Film Festival and winner of several awards), wants to see her as the heroine of his next film, *De rouille et d'os*. It is a new project that fills her with joy.

> "I never imagined that I would one day work with Jacques Audiard. I didn't even believe that he would want to. It was therefore impossible for me to refuse such an adventure. I accepted even if this period was to be reserved for the person who shares my life. We now have choices to make about not working at the same time. I could not refuse James Gray either[244]."

241. *Madame Figaro*, n° 20920, November 5, 2011.
242. He was responsible for *Le Beau Serge* (1959), *Les Cousins* (1959), *Le Boucher* (1970), *Une affaire de femmes* (1988), *La Cérémonie* (1995), *Merci pour le chocolat* (2000).
243. *Version Femina* n° 475, May 9, 2011.
244. *Madame Figaro*, n° 20920, November 5, 2011.

These latest contracts are further proof of the actress' recent international fame, which has enjoyed a meteoric rise.

During the summer of 2011, the actress settled in the city of Pittsburgh, Pennsylvania, where the entire team of *The Dark Knight Rises* is installed since July 29. It is in this Gotham City that Marion Cotillard makes her appearance (on August [1]) to play Miranda Tate, one of the members of the board of directors of Wayne Enterprises - Bruce Wayne being the real identity of "Batman, the Batman", played by Christian Bale. Although Marion Cotillard has very few shooting days, her work is spread over four months.

She follows quickly, but in the discreet, with the film of Audiard, because officially she is still shooting in Los Angeles. It is an article published in *Variety* (September 7, 2011) that revealed the "pot aux roses", with more fear than harm for our actress who finally did not suffer reprisals from the production of *Batman*.

> "My contract with Warner prevented me from acting in another film. If I left California, I could be called back at any time, which is what happened twice. This Audiard film, I really made a place for it by pushing the walls of Gotham City, the city of Batman. When I arrived in Antibes, I had just a few days to work with the orcas in Marineland. I was terrified, exhausted, I had my

baby to breastfeed... All along the shoot, I dealt with my fatigue, I used it, there was no other way. I fell asleep absolutely everywhere[245]."

Thanks to her audacity, Marion Cotillard can play Stéphanie, an orca trainer at Marineland d'Antibes who is deprived of the use of her legs after a terrible accident. The shooting of this film, which began on October 4, 2011, will last eight weeks, including 26 days on the French Riviera. Highly anticipated by moviegoers, this adaptation of Craig Davidson's short story collection[246] is already announced for the upcoming Cannes Film Festival.

Steven Soderbergh's *Contagion is* released shortly thereafter on November 9, 2011. This oppressive thriller follows a devastating pandemic exploding across the globe. Kate Winslet, Matt Damon, Jude Law, Gwyneth Paltrow and Laurence Fishburne, all great actors, are in the adventure with Marion Cotillard. She plays the role of Dr. Leonora Orantes, a European doctor who works for the World Health Organization, charged with tracking down Patient Zero in Asia.

"Before the filming, I had to talk to specialists of the O.M.S. to immerse myself in terrifying

---

245. *Télérama* n° 3252, May 12, 2012.
246. Craig DAVIDSON, *A Taste of Rust and Bone*, translated from English by Anne Wicke, collection "Terres d'Amérique", Albin Michel, Paris, 2006.

cases of new viruses that I would call "the invisible enemies". If I already had a bit of a paranoid side to these issues, this thriller exacerbated it[247]."

If we can easily imagine that the subject resonated in Marion Cotillard, concerned about the environment, the actress first chose *Contagion* for Soderbergh, a filmmaker who intrigues her: "I see him as a perfect mix between the artist and the craftsman. He writes, he shoots, he also does the lighting on the set. That may sound abstract to someone who doesn't know how film works, but imagine a kitchen or a company where one man holds all the positions[248]."

According to the newspaper *Le Monde*, the "evening" newspaper: "Soderbergh, who can flirt with virtuosity, sticks to a sober, cold staging[249]" which froze the blood of nearly 690,000 spectators in France, thus registering a semi-failure for the director (formerly Palme d'Or at the Cannes Film Festival in 1989 for *Sex, Lies and Video*, and the 2001 Oscar for best director for *Traffic*).

Marion Cotillard is indeed concerned about the future of our planet, and this since her early childhood: "I was raised by parents who were very

247. lexpress.fr, May 10, 2011.
248. *Madame Figaro*, n° 20920, November 5, 2011.
249. lemonde.fr, November 8, 2011, Thomas Sotinel.

conscious of the environment and, when I was little, I yelled at people who threw papers in the street[250]. This anger unfortunately continued to grow, to the point that it seemed impossible for her to give birth in that "world."

> "And then I met members of Greenpeace, because I wanted to get involved and do something for others. At the first meeting, I told them about my fear of having children. They told me that on the contrary, I had to have children one day so that they could continue my fight later on, and that opened my eyes[251]."

Indeed, for many years, Marion has never failed to recall her commitment to the environment during her interviews, while promoting her films as a professional.

Here is an excerpt from her open letter published in the women's magazine *Elle* n° 3295, February 21, 2009, showing a strong and sincere commitment:

> "Dear women, dear men, we have great powers, the power to destroy unconsciously, to cause the degradation of our environment, and therefore our own. We also have the power to stop destroying. For with great power comes great responsibility..."

....

250. *Gala*, n° 535, September 10, 2003.
251. marieclaire.fr, 2005.

The actress is strongly committed to the defense of the environment and human rights, especially with Greenpeace[252]. After meeting the group in 2001[253], she joined them in 2002 for her first militant act and became publicly one of the "Guardians of the Ancient Forests". In 2004, she refused to be the muse of a luxury cosmetics brand - L'Oreal - because she was on the Greenpeace *blacklist* and not in line with her commitment. In June 2010, she spent a week in the heart of the tropical forests of the Democratic Republic of Congo (DRC) with members of Greenpeace to deliver a strong testimony on the plundering of the Congolese forests which benefits a few industrial groups, often European, on video.[254]

Marion Cotillard is also the godmother of the Maud Fontenoy Foundation, which aims to protect the ocean environment. We remember that, accompanied by the famous sailor[255] and Jean-Louis Borloo (then Minister of Ecology), she came

252. The NGO Greenpeace was founded in 1970. It now fights for the protection of the environment in more than 40 countries around the world.
253. At the time, the actress had just finished shooting the second episode of *Taxi*.
254. Seven films, showing Marion Cotillard's meeting with the victims of this plundering, can be seen on the website "Congo, Forests on borrowed time".
255. Maud Fontenoy was the first woman to row across the Pacific Ocean in 2005.

- on October 8, 2010 - to present a kit on marine biodiversity in the Parisian school Valmy. "On the planet, everything is linked, the trees, the oceans, us[256]", she said. We also remember our two "fighters" on the front page of *Paris Match*[257], joining forces "in the service of the planet", in December 2010. However, nine months before, they only knew each other through the press. It was Jean-Louis Borloo who brought them together at a lunch organized for International Women's Day. "La Cotillard" was fascinated by the "icon of the seas": "Everything she said was powerful and beautiful. And accessible to all[258]." But Maud, with a touch of humour, observed Marion while talking: "I was also fascinated! I had taken her for a star who lived in a very distant world and I had even wondered if her ecological commitment was not a pose[259]."

Obviously not.

Obviously, Marion Cotillard feels some repulsion to go to a place where animals are in captivity. But the film *Rust and Bone* brought her there, in the Marineland of Antibes, playing an orca trainer.

"I never go to the zoo or even visit an aquarium. Even though I knew what I was going to

256. *Paris Match*, n° 3213, December 16, 2010.
257. *Paris Match*, n° 3213 of December 16, 2010.
258. *Ibid.*
259. *Ibid.*

be up against, I really played against my beliefs
at first[260]."

This did not prevent the actress from feeling a very strong connection with the animals. Jacques Audiard will even affirm to have been very impressed by her ease.

But Marion Cotillard is successful and leading her brilliant career, she is angry that she does not honor her commitments to them. Especially since having a child has increased this commitment. "You ask yourself different questions when you become a parent. You're more sensitive to those questions when someone depends on you, when you make choices for them[261]," she says.

Like Brigitte Bardot, who gave up cinema in 1973 to defend the animal cause, Marion Cotillard does not prevent anyone from dedicating herself to a cause and leads her career and her commitment to the planet at the same time. In September 2011, she supported the Amerindian chief Raoni Metuktire, opposed to the Belo Monte dam project (Brazil) which threatened the Amazon rainforest.

260. *Elle*, No. 3463, May 11, 2012.
261. *Glamour*, #100, July 2012.

*O*F RUST AND BONE

January 2012, New York. "The Cotillard" is in front of James Gray's camera. The director has written for her the lead role of a Polish immigrant, just arrived in the United States, who is forced to sell her body in exchange for medicine and food to support her sick sister. The situation of the young woman changes with the arrival of a magician, played by Jeremy Renner *(Minesweeper*[262]*)*, who, falling in love with the beautiful woman in distress, will do everything to save her.

This dark drama is set in the New York immigration era of 1920.

Marion Cotillard's American career never ceases to amaze, especially since there is a rapprochement between the director and the couple Canet-Cotillard: James Gray and Guillaume Canet have written together the screenplay of the American remake of *Blood ties* (in which Guillaume Canet offered a small role to Marion Cotillard).

262. *American* film by Kathryn Bigelow, released in 2009.

> "I love this city, and it has been fundamental in my professional life. This is where I shot *Nine*, this is where I got into the Oscar race, and this is where I came as a young girl to do a total immersion internship at Berlitz[263]…"

Another project is announced for mid-October and will mark his return to France: *The Past*, alongside Tahar Rahim, which is the next film of Iranian director Asghar Farhadi, with French actors.

***

On April 7, 2012, Marion Cotillard visits her compatriot Florence Cassez (37) in the women's prison of Tepepan, south of Mexico City. If since her imprisonment in December 2005 the young woman from Lille has always claimed her innocence, she was sentenced to 60 years in prison for participating in kidnappings and belonging to an organized crime network.

This information was revealed by the Mexican daily *Reforma*, and confirmed to A.F.-P. by telephone, by Florence Cassez herself: "She was the one who came forward to my support committee in France. I contacted her by phone for the first time on January 25, 2012, to thank her[264]."

263. *Elle*, No. 3463, May 11, 2012.
264. lefigaro.fr, May 1, 2012.

The imprisoned Frenchwoman, however, denied *Reforma*'s claim that during this visit a film project about her story in which Marion Cotillard would play the role of Florence Cassez was discussed.

According to the inmate[265], still at A.F.-P.: "It was a very nice meeting."

***

On May 16, 2012, dressed by Dior and adorned by Chopard, Marion Cotillard opens the 65th Cannes Film Festival, alongside director Jacques Audiard and his partner Matthias Schoenaerts. It is for them a successful entry into the competition, *De rouille et d'os* being greeted by a *standing ovation at the* end of its screening, moving its heroine. However, it did not convince the jury[266] chaired by the Italian actor-director Nanni Moretti, insensitive to this film, black as always with Audiard, and full of lyricism.

This disappointment is offset by the critical reception, including that of *Studio Ciné Live*[267]: "Carried by the mastery of its direction, *De rouille*

265. She will be released on January 23, 2013 following the cancellation for procedural defects of her conviction by the Supreme Court of Mexico.
266. The jury preferred to highlight the talent of the two actresses Cosmina Stratan and Cristina Flutur for their role in *Beyond the Hills* by Romanian director Cristian Mungiu.
267. No. 38, June 2012.

et d'os restores the often overused word emotion to its rightful place. Until now, Audiard's films have been impressive. For the first time, one of them touches us. Deeply. Powerfully. Ineffaceable." Thierry Chèze, an early fan, writes further "Marion Cotillard confirms that she is one of the greatest French actresses: her acting stripped of all effect, almost without screams or tears, is incredibly poignant." "This is perhaps Marion Cotillard's most beautiful role," writes Anne Diatkine for *Elle*[268]. "Her character is the anti-Piaf: the actress' skin is naked, her face as clear as possible... well, we see her. The success of her interpretation is also due to the fact that Marion Cotillard never turns her character into a victim. While she plays an interchangeable beauty at the beginning, she shines more and more throughout the story. We leave the film washed out. Matthias Schoenaerts, is a revelation for the audience taking Audiard's sixth film, a box-office favorite. 1.9 million spectators turn out for this love story between a marginal boxer and a killer whale trainer deprived of her legs.

"It's a film about the strength that love gives[269]."

If the Palme d'Or is awarded to *Amour* (by Michael Haneke), *De rouille et d'os* is awarded the

---

268. No. 3463, May 11, 2012.
269. *Elle*, No. 3463, May 11, 2012.

Swann d'Or for best film at the 26th Festival de Cabourg[270] in June 2012.

After the very noticed *De rouille et d'os*, she is in July 2012 in the poster of *The Dark Knight Rises*, directed by Christopher Nolan. "It's a small role but very nice[271]." In it, she plays Miranda Tate, a Gotham City high society woman, fascinated by Bruce Wayne /Batman, who dreams of transforming Gotham into a city using renewable energy. "Batman is an absolute fantasy for me. He's my favorite superhero[272]," she adds. So imagine her reaction when she learned that Nolan wanted to write her a role in the sequel to *The Dark Knight*[273], then her disappointment when she learned that the shooting dates coincided with the arrival of her "happy event".

> "And then Christopher made it all possible by moving my shooting dates to the end of June. I think that's an incredible gesture[274]..."

---

270. This year, the jury awarded the Swann d'Or for best actress to Léa Seydoux for *Les Adieux à la reine* by Benoît Jacquot and *L'Enfant d'en haut* by Ursula Meier.
271. *Version Femina*, #529, May 21, 2012.
272. *Studio Ciné Live*, #38, June 2012.
273. The saga of Christopher Nolan has a total of three parts. The first is *Batman Begins*, released in 2005, and *The Dark Knight*, released in 2008.
274. *Studio Ciné Live*, #38, June 2012.

This gesture allows him to appear in the credits of the eighth "biggest global box office success[275]" of all time. In France, *The Dark Knight Rises* made 4.4 million admissions.

The only hitch is the scene where Miranda Tate dies: judged ridiculous by a large number of spectators, the agony of her character becomes the laughing stock of Internet users and a new game, "how to die like Marion Cotillard", makes the happiness of the Web, making of her an "e-target", an object of endless mockery.

Faced with this huge *buzz*, Guillaume Canet takes his defense: "All this story about the sequence where the character of Marion dies in *The Dark Knight Rises* is absolutely not his fault," regrets Guillaume.

> "It's Nolan's, who should have done another take. She gave him a lot of options, and he happened to choose that one... I think it's very brave of an actor to offer so many different takes to a director. Afterwards, it's up to him to be vigilant when he's facing his film on the editing bench[276]."

275. After, in order: 7. *Skyfall* (2012); 6. *The Lord of the Rings: The Return of the King* (2003); 5. *Transformers 3: The Dark Side of the Moon* (2011); 4. *Harry Potter and the Deathly Hallows: Part 2* (2011); 3. *Avengers* (2012); 2. *Titanic* (1997); 1. *Avatar* (2009).
276. *Premiere*, No. 430, December 2012 / January 2013.

Anyway, we still laugh about it for a long time: in an episode of *Plus belle la vie*[277], scheduled on France 3, January 9, 2014, Valentin, Laurie, Emilie and Greg go to the movies and debate Marion Cotillard's acting before imitating said scene!

Marion Cotillard's response to the *"Dark Knight Rises"* affair was in Cambridge, where she was elected Woman of the Year by the Harvard Hasty Pudding, the theater club of the famous university, where as tradition dictates, after attending a parade surrounded by *drag queens*, the distinguished guest acted out some of the highlights of her filmography, including one in which she dies in Miranda Tate expressions.

If this January 31, 2013 the French actress received a special honor, she did leave this burlesque ceremony with the Pudding Pot and a wide smile.

Her sense of humor has hit home, as in March 2010, for International Women's Day. In a video, *Forehead Tittaes*, published on *funnyordie.com* (the website of actor Will Ferrell, specializing in parody) Marion Cotillard then displayed breasts on the forehead to denounce macho behavior! A very effective humoristic strategy, especially from a Dior muse.

277. Niseema Theillaud, Marion Cotillard's mother, played the character of Madame Tressere - from April 2011 to February 2012 - in this television drama that often triggers peak ratings.

That said, Marion Cotillard did see the said scene, which gave her "a kind of mini-depression[278]". In general, she sees her films once or twice. She needs it to work, to analyze herself. "After that, my opinion is my own[279]," she says. Then, she never sees them again, because Marion is afraid of being bad. "Despite my Oscar, I'm still afraid of not being up to par," she confided, not long ago, to *Paris Match*[280], which crowned her "Star" of Cannes 2012. Marion Cotillard is the first to say, "I've shot films in which I'm not good at all[281]." This couac was disproportionate: but to be a star today is also to unleash the Internet users and inspire them pastiches of all kinds.

De rouille et d'os brought her a more glorious harvest of awards, including a prize for best actress at the Hollywood and Hawaii Film Festivals, as well as the Crystal Globe and the Golden Star for best actress. However, the César[282] goes to Emmanuelle Riva (85 years old), who won several awards for Haneke's *Amour*, including the Italian Online Movie Award, ex æquo with Marion Cotillard.

---

278. *Ouest France*, November 25, 2013.
279. *Version Femina*, n° 475, May 9, 2011.
280. No. 3288, May 24, 2012.
281. *Paris Match*, No. 3288, May 24, 2012.
282. Out of nine nominations, *De rouille et d'os* won four César awards, including the one for best male hopeful awarded to Matthias Schoenaerts.

For his part, the most coveted French director of the moment, Jacques Audiard, praises his interpreter of *Rust and Bone*: "After writing the script of *Rust and Bone*, when it came to choosing the actors, Marion's name came to me very quickly. Why did you choose her? Because of the way she commits herself totally, entirely to the game. You only have to see her in *La Môme*: very few actresses are capable of giving what she gave. With her, it's about self-surrender, she throws herself into a state, without psychology, in a very physical way. However, she is also very rational: before playing a scene, she wonders about the meaning of the gestures, the movements or the words, she asks for clear and especially logical indications. But, once this rational base is there, she gives herself up body and soul, with an immoderate power. With her, each first take is an explosion[283]".

> "In fact, it was after the shooting that I think he appreciated me. He probably understood that I regretted not having been able to bring him, during the rehearsals, what he wanted. We must be similar. With him, you don't always know where you're going, but when you get there, you feel it... I hate disappointing my director: my dream, each time, is to dive into his universe to try to find,

283. *Psychologies Magazine*, No. 319, June 2012.

with him, some pieces of authenticity. Everything else is useless. Superfluous[284]...”

The main thing is that *De rouille et d'os* has put Marion Cotillard back into the world of French cinema:

“Marion proved that she could return very naturally to French cinema. And that was her greatest challenge: not to cut herself off from the cinema and the country that are hers,” said Thierry Frémeaux, general delegate of the Cannes Film Festival. “She never gave the impression that she lived anywhere but in France. Audiard offered her the perfect role for this[285].”

284. *Télérama*, No. 3357, May 17, 2014.
285. *L'Express*, No. 3228, May 15, 2013.

The Dardenne brothers

Marion Cotillard, who does not lack work, decided to take a break.

> "I don't have time to do nothing, to dream. I need it. I'm offered exciting projects, it's hard to refuse. But now I've decided that in the next few months I'm going to put my foot down. I know that I will have to give up some great offers. But I want to spend time with my family[286].

In fact, she turned down her role in *Le Passé* at the last minute in favor of Bérénice Bejo, the unforgettable Peppy Miller of *The Artist*[287].

But she doesn't want to stop: "No, I like acting so much, giving life to characters... Maybe one day it will stop, but for the moment, it is too important a motor in my life. It just takes too much time. Or I don't know how to manage it well, that's my problem[288]."

286. *Paris Match*, No. 3288, May 24, 2012.
287. César for the best actress in 2012 for Bérénice Bejo.
288. *Psychology Magazine*, No. 319 - June 2012.

For Guillaume Canet, the day after his breakup with Diane Kruger: "At a certain level of involvement in this business, you end up neglecting your personal life[289]." For her part, Marion Cotillard says: "If a man asks me one day to stop the cinema, it is because he will not love me anymore." But she adds: "If there were only my roles, nothing would rhyme[290].

The French actress has not disappeared from the stage for all that. She made a return to the theater on November 17 and 18, 2012, at the Barcelona Auditorium, to play *Joan of Arc at the stake*, accompanied by the Barcelona and National Symphony Orchestra of Catalonia, conducted by Marc Soustrot[291]. Marion Cotillard dreamed of doing it again.

"Jeanne is a passionate person like me, she follows her instincts, she has faith in existence[292]."

A revival of this oratorio was aborted in July 2009. It was planned at the Marigny theater in Paris, with choirs and musicians who were to be directed by the conductor Jean-Marc Cochereau. He left us in January 2011.

289. *Paris Match*, n° 3048, October 18, 2007.
290. *Paris Match*, n° 3048, October 18, 2007.
291. Xavier Gallais played the role of Brother Dominique.
292. lemonde.fr, March 20, 2015.

Then we saw her on Canal+ in *Le Débarquement*, broadcast in January 2013, showing her as the introverted wife of Mr. Picot (Guillaume Canet). At first she looks like a bear who, consulting a plastic surgeon (Gilles Lellouche), metamorphoses, after the operation, into a hairy Marion Cotillard who growls, rolls around on the floor and eats honey right out of the jar. Marion Cotillard, who has not accustomed his audience to such pranks, allows himself a recreation.

During this 2013, Marion Cotillard has once again been shooting alongside high-profile directors. According to *Variety*, she is set to play Celestine in *Le Journal d'une femme de chambre*, Benoît Jacquot's adaptation of Octave Mirbeau's novel - a golden role previously held by Paulette Goddard (in 1946) and Jeanne Moreau (in 1964). The prospect of this filming, which will begin in the spring of 2014, delights them both.

A press release from the French production company Archipel 35 later announced that she would be starring in Jean-Pierre and Luc Dardenne's next film, *Two Days, One Night*, which began shooting in the Liège region in the summer of 2013. Note that it is rare that the Dardenne brothers choose a very well-known actress:

> "Yes, for sure when my agent told me that
> they were thinking about me for a movie, I was

surprised. I never thought I would get an offer from them. At our first meeting, it was borderline overwhelming[293]."

What's more, Marion could soon appear in another big production that we are looking forward to: the remake of *La Balance* by Florent Emilio-Siri. Indeed, the director of *Cloclo is currently* developing a retelling of Bob Swain's film, released in 1982, which will be produced by Thomas Langmann *(The Artist)*. Marion would take over the role of Nicole, the prostitute previously played by Nathalie Baye, who was awarded the César for best actress in 1983.

She also made a surprise appearance in the spring of 2013 in the sultry video clip of the song of David Bowie *The Next Day,* directed by Floria Sigismondi. We then admire a Marion Cotillard, in the role of a prostitute, dancing alongside a priest, played by the British actor Gary Oldman. She then reappears as a madonna, behind a David Bowie looking like a guru. Decadent atmosphere guaranteed: the controversy is aroused.

To be contacted by David Bowie is not something trivial:

> "One day, I received an e-mail with the subject line: "David Bowie and Marion Cotillard". I thought it was a joke! But he proposed me to play

293. *Marie Claire*, #742, June 2014.

in his clip and sent me the synopsis. Bowie has an incomparable class, he sings wonderfully, he has rock in his soul. The video caused an immediate controversy. When David Bowie creates a scandal, it is worn with pride[294]."

And it pays off! After a ten-year absence, the eventful album *The Next Day*, marks the return of the "greatest comeback album in the history of rock". Prepared in the greatest secrecy, this twenty-fourth studio album of David Bowie is unanimously acclaimed by the critics and certified platinum in France.

Also the song plays a very important role in the life of the French actress:

> "I would like to devote more time to music. But I've got it in my head to write my own lyrics. And as I take two years to write a song, I am not close to release an album. For a long time I thought I was incapable of writing, I didn't feel legitimate, but I love music[295]."

***

At Cannes, on May 20, 2013, Marion Cotillard appears in *Blood Ties*, a film out of competition by Guillaume Canet. On the 24th, she is also in

---

294. *L'Express*, No. 3255, November 20, 2013.
295. *Ouest France*, November 25, 2013.

competition for *The Immigrant*, by James Gray. Both have given her a role as an exile who prostitutes herself to survive. She plays an Italian immigrant from New York in the first and a Polish woman with a Silesian accent in the second. Two characters with impeccable tones.

> "I have no choice if I want to be credible. Language reflects the history and culture of a country. It's also a question of respect for the Italians and the Poles. For *Blood Ties,* I had to assimilate that *groove* between Italian and New York typical of Scorsese's films of the 1970s... And, for *The Immigrant,* I raided the Polish Bookstore in Paris, and watched a lot of films to hear the language. I remember answering James, who asked me about my slight German accent in my Polish lines: "It's done on purpose because my character comes from Silesia, a region located between Germany and Poland[296]".

Marion Cotillard is also very sensitive to the situation of migrants today: "When I was little, my mother took me to Amnesty International meetings: a small office with five people trying to save lives. It's striking[297]."

> "The driving force behind my choices is never the challenge. I have an immense desire to explore

296. *L'Express*, No. 3255, November 20, 2013.
297. *Elle*, No. 3542, November 15, 2013.

> but I will never say "yes" if I feel that I don't belong in an adventure. Even to Guillaume I didn't say "yes" right away. James Gray, it is different. He warned me that he was writing a role for me and I was overexcited. He is modest and sensitive, but he is someone who knows what he wants: he got to shoot on Ellis Island, the landing place for immigrants, in New York. Even Coppola[298] didn't get permission[299]!"

However, the jury chaired by Steven Spielberg awarded the Palme d'Or of the 66th Cannes Film Festival to the film *La Vie d'Adèle*, by Abdellatif Kechiche, which deals with the burning passion between two women (played by Adèle Exarchopoulos and Léa Seydoux) and the Best Actress Award went instead to Bérénice Bejo for her role in *Le Passé*.

Marion Cotillard does not think that she made a mistake in choosing James Gray over Asghar Farhadi: "The roles come when you are ready to receive them, to make them live[300]. In addition, it is not in her habit to jealously watch her competitors:

---

298. Allusion to the beginning of the film *Godfather II* by Francis Ford Coppola (released in 1974) and the arrival of the little Corleone and other Italian emigrants at Ellis Island.
299. *Ouest France*, November 25, 2013.
300. *Télérama*, No. 3252, May 12, 2012.

> "In any case, I'm not one to fight for the top
> spot. If someone wants it, they can take it easily,
> and I'll take a back seat[301]."

For his new film, James Gray, who always left Cannes empty-handed[302], claims the genre of melodrama through these two Polish sisters who emigrated to New York in the 1920s, whose story is inspired by the memories of his own Ukrainian immigrant grandparents who came to New York in 1923. For him, there was no doubt about the casting, it was Marion Cotillard. He wrote the script for her and would not have made the film without her. "Unfortunately, I haven't seen any of her films, but when I met her at a dinner with Guillaume Canet, with whom I was working on the adaptation of *Blood Ties*, I immediately liked her face, the quality and depth of her expressions. I thought of the image of Carl Dreyer's *Joan of Arc*[303]. She could very well do silent films. It is very rare for an actor or actress to express so much feeling without sometimes saying a word[304]."

301. *Studio Magazine*, n° 215, September 2005.
302. Before *The Immigrant*, James Gray had already three films selected at the Cannes Film Festival (*The Yards* in 2000, *La nuit nous appartient* in 2007 and *Two Lovers* in 2008).
303. *The Passion of Joan of Arc*, a film by Carl Theodor Dreyer, released in 1927 with Renee Falconetti in the title role.
304. *Le Figaro*, May 26, 2013.

This is the reason for this (very nice) review, signed by Pierre Murat for *Télérama*[305]:

> "The face of a woman. In this church where she has taken refuge to abandon herself, at last, to grief, James Gray films Marion Cotillard like a heroine of tragedy, suddenly welcoming in herself a grace she no longer hopes for. Like a silent film star, too: she looks like Lillian Gish in some of Griffith's melos. Beauty in its purest form... During the long time that this magnificent shot lasts, we contemplate this woman in distress, illuminated by the light of candles and a choir of voices that seem, for a moment, to soothe her..."

Indeed, as a young Polish woman whose arrival in the land promised to the starry banner is not under the best auspices, "the Cotillard" is "literally overwhelming[306]". "She holds her role beautifully[307]." A character that, in the absence of the Cannes award, will earn him honors including the United States (New York Film Critics Circle / Boston Society of Film Critics / National Society of Film Critics[308]) and in Canada (Toronto Film Critics Association).

---

305. No. 3333, November 30, 2013.
306. *The Utopia Gazette*, No. 201, November 6, 2013.
307. Éric Neuhoff, *Le Figaro*, November 27, 2013.
308. Ex aequo three times with herself for her interpretation of Sandra in *Two Days, One Night*, by the Dardenne brothers.

However, the enthusiasm of the French public is more moderate. Released on November 27, 2013, *The Immigrant* only mobilized 322,576 spectators. A regrettable score, because James Gray considers it his best film - along with *Two Lovers* - because he laid his emotions bare, "without distance, without restraint, without the slightest veil between the film and the viewer[309]."

The film *Blood Ties*, in theaters October 30, 2013, coldly received by critics, will not meet the enthusiasm of the public either. 238,823 French viewers turned out for the replay (rather than remake) of Jacques Maillot's *Blood Ties*[310]. The film transposes, in the America of 1974, the relationship between two brothers that everything opposes, except the blood that runs in their veins. One is a cop (Billy Crudup), the other a "hothead" just out of prison. Marion Cotillard plays his ex-wife, who fights for her own survival and above all for that of her two children. "It has become one of my favorite characters in my career[311]," she admits. "In fact, it was my idea that Monica, my character, could be

309. *Télérama*, No. 3333, November 30, 2013.
310. Released in 2008, with Guillaume Canet, François Cluzet and Carole Franck, and respectively in *Blood Ties* Billy Crudup, Clive Owen and Marion Cotillard. Box office for Blood Ties: 513,059 admissions.
311. *Télé 7 jours*, No. 2851, January 17, 2015.

Italian. That was before I remembered that I don't speak a word of Italian[312]..."

In short, it is "a dark and nostalgic thriller whose images remain engraved on the retina, like the small dust encrusted on the sapphire of a hi-fi system of the 1970s[313]...".

***

Shot shortly after the release of *Bood Ties, Two Days, One Night was* filmed entirely in Belgium, in Seraing, like all the films of the Dardenne brothers.

> "The shoot was everything I ever dreamed of. No words are enough. All of a sudden, the question of why you want to be an actress no longer arises. Because it's for this kind of unique experience that you choose to be[314]."

Cherished by the Americans, adopted by the Belgians, it seems to us that the culture shock must have been disorienting.

> "Not so much: there are fries on the menu in both cases! More seriously, when you talk about Hollywood, people think money and *glamour*. And when you talk about the Dardennes, they think of "boring" and "gray" auteur cinema. But

312. *Le Figaro*, October 30, 2013.
313. Olivier DELCROIX *Le Figaro*, October 30, 2013.
314. *Elle*, No. 3542,November 15, 2013.

they are wrong in both cases: the Dardennes are exciting and suspenseful. And since they only make one film every three years, they have the human and economic means to do it well! On the other hand, I've made films that are broke in Hollywood: James Gray's *The Immigrant*, for example, which, contrary to appearances, was shot with very little money.

And you have to beware of appearances: I spent more time in the hands of the hairdresser on the set of the Dardenne brothers than on many American films. To achieve a badly done, but fitting ponytail, every day, it's a sport[315]."

While she was shooting this film, the fiancée of French cinema, Bernadette Lafont[316], passed away on July 25, 2013, at the age of 74.

"The announcement of her death made for a particularly difficult day on the Dardenne brothers' film. She was singular and funny, and had a unique way of looking at the profession, with a great distance and an intensity that never wavered. She gave me this founding sentence: "In this profession, you will meet a lot of people who will tell you that you are the eighth wonder of the world. Consider them just saying hello. A book that I love and that guides me, *The Four Toltec Agreements*, by Don Miguel Ruiz, goes along the same

315. *Grazia*, No. 241, May 9, 2014.
316. *The heroine of* Le Beau Serge *(1958),* La Fiancée du pirate *(1969),* Une belle fille comme moi *(1972),* La Maman et la Putain *(1973),* Paulette *(2013), etc.*

lines. One of these agreements enjoins us to take nothing personally. To welcome the good and the bad with distance[317]."

Since this shooting, Marion Cotillard is preparing to take on a new challenge: playing Lady Macbeth opposite the German-Irish actor Michael Fassbender in *Macbeth* by the Australian Justin Kurzel, based on the great classic by William Shakespeare. With this latest project, she confirms that her life as an actress is an artistic adventure without limits and a delightful French exception. However, the actress keeps a certain humility:

> "I amaze myself... but only in the kitchen. I'm very good at risotto. Other than that, it's very rare for me to get amazed. Sometimes I think I did the best I could, and it shows on the screen a little. I feel like I'm starting over with every film. Even though I'm starting to have the background to be able to get into certain emotions a little faster. I'm lucky enough to receive proposals from directors I admire and who inspire me. I find that miraculous[318]."

*****

Paris, November 15, 2013. Marion Cotillard and French political and cultural figures symbolically

317. *Le Nouvel Observateur*, No. 2583, May 8, 2014.
318. *Ouest France*, November 25, 2013.

put themselves in cages to show their support for the "30 of the Arctic[319]," a Greenpeace activist group detained for two months in Russia for trying to delay Russian oil drilling in the Barents Sea in the Arctic. According to Vladimir Putin, they have "violated the law of the sea[320]". On the other hand, Marion Cotillard told the press: "There are people who have the courage to defend our planet, which is really being harmed. Faced with this courage, the sanctions incurred are absolutely absurd and crazy... We should rather thank these people[321]."

After several years of support for Greenpeace, Marion Cotillard is still questioning, again and again.

> "Recently, I've been wondering a lot about whether, when I speak out publicly in support of a cause or association, it can really make a difference. Does it really help? Is it worth it? Wangari Maathai, Aung San Suu Kyi, Nelson Mandela have made a difference. But, actors and stars, I don't know. Maybe... Maybe I don't give enough time to the people I support. Sometimes I feel like I should choose between acting and supporting a cause[322]."

319. The "Arctic 30" were released and amnestied on December 18, 2013, after a major international public mobilization in their favor.
320. southwest.com, November 2, 2014.
321. lefigaro.fr, November 15, 2013.
322. *Marie Claire*, #722, October 2012.

Then, after having been a member of the short film jury in 2002, as a member of the feature film jury, presided over by Martin Scorsese *(Taxi Driver, Casino, The Wolf of Wall Street)*, the fervent supporter of Greenpeace returned to the backstage of the Marrakech International Film Festival[323].

The international actress meets on the *red carpet* Sylvie Testud, whom she had not seen for a long time, but to whom she offers a huge smile when she sees her a little further away, not daring to advance towards her - Cotillard is expected by a cloud of photographers shouting her name louder than any other. Finally the one who played Mômone, Piaf's best friend in *La Môme*, advances: "Hi, Sylvie. Martin, this is Sylvie Testud, Sylvie, this is Martin Scorsese[324].

Unquestionably, Marion Cotillard has become a star. Later, Sylvie Testud questions the one for whom life and career have taken an exceptional turn, precisely since the release of *La Môme*: "Aren't you afraid when these directors call you?" "I'm terrified," she answers. I'm afraid of disappointing them, so I work like crazy[325].

---

323. This thirteenth edition takes place from November 29 to December 7, 2013.
324. *Madame Figaro*, No. 21696, May 9, 2014.
325. *Madame Figaro*, No. 21696, May 9, 2014.

Marion Cotillard did not take the big head. Except that already, "[she] worked 15 hours a day. Every day," recalls Sylvie Testud when they were shooting Dahan's film.

A true workaholic who walks in the absolute, the gift of self, Marion Cotillard, without question, dominates: she is elected "most beautiful face of 2013" by the American website *TC Candler*. An envied title.

David Lynch, the illusionist of the big screen and confirmed aesthete, declares: " I had seen Marion in *La Môme*, but I had not realized how much she is very beautiful, very stylish[326].

Cotillard-Lynch: it is the "ticket" for the least explosive gathered in December 2009 by Dior for the advertising short film *Lady Blue Shanghai*, shot in the Chinese megalopolis.

On the male side, it is Michael Fassbender who is at the top of the "100 most beautiful faces of men in the world", still according to *TC Candler*.

---

326. *L'Express*, n° 3071, May 12, 2010.

Macbeth and Two Days, One Night

Marion Cotillard and Michael Fassbender are actors in high demand. In 2008, Michael Fassbender had exploded on the Croisette, during the presentation of the powerful *Hunger* by Steve McQueen. This is a duo of actors for the director Justin Kurzel, who was a sensation at Cannes in 2011 with *The Crimes of Snowton*. He begins with them, February 3, 2014 and for seven weeks, the shooting of *Macbeth*, in Scotland and England.

As Lord Macbeth, Michael Fassbender may deliver one of the most visceral performances of his young career. As for Marion Cotillard as Lady Macbeth, she plays a score considered one of the most difficult in the Western repertoire. It is also the most difficult film of her entire career, whose obstacles seemed insurmountable:

"Often in interviews, people say to me, "You like to take on challenges with the films you choose to shoot!" I used to say no. On the set of *Macbeth*, I asked myself if finally the journalists were not right and if I was not unconsciously challenging myself. I couldn't do anything that hard[327]." It was crazy complex. "I think I've reached my maximum threshold from that point of view and don't wish to go any further[328]!"

About Lady Macbeth, she also states:

> "I had no control over her, and for good reason, she herself loses control and goes mad. My characters affect me. Their condition reflects on me. There, I was going completely crazy. I had to send my son back to France so that my nervousness wouldn't infect him. I am quite sane, but I felt that I could not cope. I wasn't me anymore.[...] I just hope that what I did is not going to be too rotten, even ridiculous[329]."

Then, Marion Cotillard was supposed to follow with *Le Journal d'une femme de chambre* by Benoît Jacquot, but she finally refused:

> "After *Two Days, One Night* and *Macbeth, it* was impossible for me to imagine not stopping. I do have a problem: I don't know how to take a real vacation in my head. At the end of *Two Days, One Night*, I did, but knowing that I had *Macbeth* behind me, I started thinking about the role. And, while shooting *Macbeth*, I had a real moment of panic. I needed to be alone, without a character in mind[330]!"

327. *Version Femina*, #633, May 19, 2014.
328. *Studio Ciné Live*, #59, May 2014.
329. *Le Nouvel Observateur*, No. 2583, May 8, 2014.
330. *Studio Ciné Live*, #59, May 2014.

Benoît Jacquot and Vincent Lindon were very understanding and it is finally Léa Seydoux, 28, who will take over the role.

In May 2014, once again, Marion Cotillard is a sensation in Cannes. *Two Days, One Night* represents Belgium at the 67th edition of the Festival, chaired by New Zealander Jane Campion[331]. This is the third consecutive year that she is in competition.

> "I really discovered this festival two years ago. When you are a small actress with not much to do there, you suffer in Cannes, it's too big a machine. But when you come there to defend a film, it's extraordinary[332]."

Two Days, One Night is a drama in which Marion plays Sandra, a woman who has only one weekend to convince her 13 colleagues to give up their 1,000-euro bonus so she can keep her job. She is helped by her husband, played by Fabrizio Rongione, used to work in front of the camera of the Dardenne, already Palme d'Or at Cannes for *Rosetta* and *L'Enfant*.

Participating in this filming was a real risk for Marion Cotillard and one can wonder at the time if the Dior muse will manage to immerse herself in the naturalistic universe of the Dardenne brothers.

331. Palme d'Or 1993 for his film *The Piano Lesson*.
332. *Elle*, No. 3567, May 9, 2014.

The international star, hyperglamorous on the steps of the Palace - on May 20, alongside the two Belgian filmmakers and Fabrizio Rongione - can she still erase herself for the benefit of her character? The answer is yes. She is neither Marion nor Cotillard. "This portrait of a woman in distress rests on the shoulders of her interpreter," writes Eric Neuhoff in *Le Figaro*[333]. "Cotillard" can play anything and the Dardenne brothers are admirers of the range of possibilities offered by the actress's game.

"Darrin. - She has a sense of rhythm. She vibrates... We like to change the tempo as we go along. Or ask for unexpected silences. Each time, she would invent. The actors we often work with - Olivier Gourmet, Fabrizio Rongione - know how to play with our camera, to move at the right moment, to turn around when necessary. She understood everything very quickly...

Luc. - His way of falling down, too! It's kind of our thing, the falling bodies! Seeing her spread out during the rehearsals, we were able to refine our staging to the second...

Jean-Pierre. - And then there is the hand scene. Tell us about it...

---

333. May 21, 2014 edition.

Luke. - At one point, the heroine is in full discouragement and her husband takes her hand. Suddenly, we saw Marion playing with her fingers on Fabrizio's wrist. And this gesture that she invented made moving his tiredness. And her disarray...

Jean-Pierre. - So we go to her: "Marion, this gesture, could you do it again ?" We do seven or eight takes and each time it's as beautiful as the first one...

Luc. - We are rather meticulous, but during the editing, we noticed other small inventions of Marion that we had not spotted on the set. These details that make the essential. Invisible gifts [334]..."

Julianne Moore being rewarded for David Cronenberg's *Maps to the Stars*, Marion Cotillard is, according to the general opinion, the great forgotten of the prize list - leaving to her admirers a small regret.

> You don't have to make the films for that," she says. The most important thing is that the film is seen and appreciated. It's a jury, it's also about taste. It's not like there are thousands of people voting, there are only nine [335]."

334. *Télérama*, No. 3357, May 17, 2014.
335. *Version Femina*, #633, May 19, 2014.

Opening May 21, 2014, *Two Days, One Night*, which returned from Cannes with the Ecumenical Jury Prize[336], will total 511,593 tickets sold in France.

------

336. Awarded to a film in the official competition that delivers a message by an independent jury composed of Catholics and Protestants.

A FAMILY OF ARTISTS

In Cannes in 2014, Marion Cotillard has once again caused a sensation on the red carpet of the Palais des Festivals. Guillaume Canet presented on May 21 his new film, out of competition, signed André Téchiné, *The Man We Loved Too Much*. He shares the poster with Catherine Deneuve and Adèle Haenel. Marion Cotillard supported her companion in the presence of his mother, Niseema Theillaud, now separated from Jean-Claude Cotillard.

> "She is someone extremely important in my life and whom I adore. The bravest person I know. Of course, I have also experienced complicated moments with her, as happens to all children[337]."

Marion Cotillard has two brothers, Guillaume and Quentin, with whom she was allowed to draw on the walls of their eighteenth floor apartment in Alfortville.

---

337. *Marie Claire*, #742, June 2014.

Guillaume has been making short films[338], since recently, after working in computers. His twin brother, Quentin, is a sculptor and painter based in San Francisco, California. Marion is very proud of them. The creative side of both of them, as well as Marion, has always been supported by their parents: "This is the most beautiful thing they gave me, along with the notion of respect, openness of mind and heart[339]."

On May 19, 2014, his son Marcel turned three years old. Perhaps he is a future actor who will follow in his parents' footsteps...

> "I had wonderful parents who, rather than handing us their "garbage", as we used to say in the family - or let's say the "suitcases" of their family neuroses -, raised us in total freedom, respect, curiosity, culture. They didn't freak out when I told them I wanted to be an actress. They have always supported me. I want to transmit the same thing to my son. But to see him express, one day, the desire to make this profession would tear me apart. To be a good actor, you have to have big flaws that may never be filled. On the one hand, I would start hoping that he would become a great actor. On the other hand, I would know that his desire stems from something very painful[340]."

338. *The Key to the Problem* (2008) and *By Mutual Consent* (2014).
339. lexpress.fr, May 10, 2011.
340. *Le Nouvel Observateur*, No. 2583, May 8, 2014.

Marion Cotillard remains discreet about her relationship with Guillaume Canet: "I would find it in bad taste[341] " she once confided. Her public statements about him are all related to their work together on films. However, she does not try to maintain any mystery around their relationship. Of course, it is difficult to reconcile the schedules when you are an actor couple, it is one of the difficulties of their profession.

> "The two of us do everything we can to make sure there's no frustration[342]."

Their discretion generates, on the front page of the sensationalist press in search of publicity, rumors saying they are on the verge of breaking up[343].

It is that the couple appears together only on rare occasions, as on February 20, 2015, at the 40th ceremony of the Cesar Awards. That evening, Guillaume Canet was vying for the title of "best actor[344]" for his role as an assassin above suspicion in *The Next Time I Aim for the Heart,* by Cédric Anger. Marion was nominated for her performance in *Two Days, One Night*[345].

341. *Paris Match*, n° 3170, February 18, 2010.
342. *Marie Claire*, #742, June 2014.
343. Examples: the magazine *Voici* n° 1328 of February 9, 2013, or *Public* n° 617 of May 7, 2015.
344. Winner: Pierre Niney for Yves Saint Laurent by Jalil Lespert.
345. Winner: Adèle Haenel for Les Combattants by Thomas Cailley.

Guillaume Canet, who had to give up a career as a professional rider[346], has now managed to make a place for himself in the world of cinema.

If Marion Cotillard preserves her private life, she still communicates in the press the happiness that implies her family life. "Since Marcel was born, he lights up my life every day. My family made me discover my capacity to be happy. It wasn't always the case so I know how lucky I am[347]," she said.

Flourishing, Marion Cotillard is also on glossy paper, in her simplest camera in front of the lens of her friend, photographer Eliott Bliss, to present a collection of jewelry Chopard: the result is a sensual premiere, in black and white, for the cover of Russian magazine *SNC* (November 2014).

On November 4, 2014, during a special broadcast, celebrating the 30 years of Canal+, she performs *live*, with the group Metronomy, a cover of Joe Jackson, *Is she realy going out with him?* Her performance was recorded at the Palais des Sports in Paris. It is understandable that she does not hold any grudge against the encrypted channel and its satirical *Guignols de l'Info*[348], which have repeatedly targeted her.

346. Since the film *Jappeloup* (2013), Guillaume Canet has resumed his license and practices jumping.
347. Claire FORTIN, "A French actress in the heart of Hollywood," *Jour de France*, No. 48, March 2015.
348. His puppet made its debut on February 20, 2013. It is the impersonator Sandrine Alexi who lends him his voice.

On the eve
of his 40th birthday

Marion Cotillard is where you would not expect her. In 2015 she accompanied (along with Melanie Laurent) François Hollande on a trip to the Philippines[349] to advocate against global warming. On February 26, 2015, Marion Cotillard launched the "Manila Appeal[350]" from the Philippine presidential palace to, according to the entourage of the President of the French Republic, solicit "the mobilization of all for an agreement in Paris[351]". It is the environmental activist Nicolas Hulot who is at the origin of this initiative.

A few days earlier, on February 22, 2015, Marion Cotillard went to Los Angeles and claimed the Oscar for Best Actress for *Two Days, One Night*[352]. Her

349. The Philippines is considered the most disaster-prone country in the world according to the Global Risk Index.
350. lefigaro.fr, February 24, 2015.
351. In December, the French capital will host the delegations of 196 countries for the 2015 climate conference, with the aim of reaching an ambitious agreement on reducing CO_2 consumption.
352. For this film, Marion Cotillard won multiple awards including - for the first time, on December 13, 2014 - the European Film Award for best actress.

competitors included Felicity Jones, Julianne Moore, Rosamund Pike and Reese Witherspoon. Julianne Moore won for her sensitive and moving portrayal of a woman with early onset Alzheimer's in *Still Alice*. In an interview, she praised Marion Cotillard's talent: "To tell you the truth, I think Marion Cotillard would have deserved the Oscar more than I do[353]!"

Marion Cotillard has not finished seducing the public. In Toulouse, after Monaco, she lends her voice to Joan of Arc to play again the work of Paul Claudel, *Joan of Arc at the stake*[354].

It was on the eve of the performance, February 13, 2015, that the request to write this book was made. "Is it well worth it?" she replied, naturally and without pretension.

She dreams of working with her father on stage.

> "He knows, he's waiting for me to be available.
> When I'm ready, I'll go get him[355]."

353. Hervé TROPÉA, "Julianne Moore *(Stil Alice)* : "Marion Cotillard deserved the Oscar more than me!" *(Interview)*", Télé Loisirs 15 March 2015. URL: <http://www.programme-tv.net/news/cinema/63930-julianne-moore-still-alice-marion-cotillard-aurait-merite-l-oscar-plus-que-moi-interview/>.
354. With music by Honegger, with the Orchestre national du Capitole de Toulouse, conducted by Kazuki Yamada. In August 2012, Kazuki Yamada was (already) called to conduct Joan of Arc at the stake at the Saito Kinen Festival in Japan (Joan was then Isabel Karajan).
355. "Marion Cotillard on stage in Toulouse: "Joan of Arc is sensitive is strong," *La Dépêche du Midi*, February 13, 2015.

As a child, she saw all his mime shows, which fed her imagination.

> "He taught me the basics of this discipline. I can pretend to be stuck by a wall. I can ride a bike without a bike, eat apples without an apple, climb stairs without stairs[356]..."

For Jean-Claude Cotillard, her father, "if Marion is what she is, it is not because she wanted to go to the end of the world. But because she sought to go to the end of herself. In his eyes, this is the only interesting thing in life[357]..."

But before reaching *the end of herself*, Marion Cotillard will be in the cast of the next film by Quebec director Xavier Dolan *(Mommy)*, entitled *Just the end of the world*[358], based on a play written by Jean-Luc Lagarce.

She will also begin shooting[359] of Nicole Garcia's new film[360], an adaptation of the bestseller *Mal de pierres* by Milena Agus.

----

356. Paola GENONE, "Marion Cotillard: "I would have loved to walk up the steps with Woody Allen," lexpress.fr, May 10, 2011.
357. Dany JUCAUD, "Marion Cotillard. La belle Américaine", *Paris Match*, n° 3170, 18 February 2010.
358. Shooting from May 27 to June 28, 2015.
359. June 29, 2015.
360. Nicole Garcia had already proposed him *A balcony on the sea*, released in December 2010, with Jean Dujardin and Marie-Josée Croze.

Then she will join Justin Kurzel to star in the highly anticipated adaptation of the video game *Assassin's Creed*, with Michael Fassbender.

At the same time, *Macbeth*[361] was selected for Cannes in 2015 where she presented an "eco-responsible hand jewel" by Swiss jeweler Chopard.

***

For the continuation, Marion Cotillard has desires of change.

> "I dream of playing in a comedy, because it touches the audience more than tragedies. And I would also love to play a man[362]!"

***

Marion Cotillard celebrates her fortieth birthday on September 30, 2015 and says, "All I can say is that I have always lived every step of my life to the fullest[363]."

---

361. *Macbeth* will be released in France on November 18, 2015. And if Marion Cotillard, bloody Lady Macbeth, will be praised by the critics, the film, although spectacular, will be a failure on the box office side, with 88,378 hexagonal entries.
362. lecho.be, 11 May 2015.
363. Paola GENONE, "Marion Cotillard: "I would have loved to walk up the steps with Woody Allen," lexpress.fr, May 10, 2011.

And unlike Marilyn Monroe, she does not fear the weight of the years, neither in her career[364], nor in her life. On the contrary, she lives in the present time, wonders about the future of the planet[365] but does not worry about her age:

> "It's horrible these expressions "she took a blow of old", "she is typed"… I hear them as well in Paris as in Hollywood. For the moment, I cling to my good genes! And I have the chance to be a phobic of injections.
> Frankly, I hope I will accept my wrinkles rather than live in fear of them. But how do I know? It's so complex[366]!"

She will be remembered for having crossed borders. "I wanted to be an actress. I didn't want to be a French actress[367]" declared, one day, the one who doesn't do this job to be someone else but on the contrary "to experience the human soul, to try to understand how it all works, to simply want to be

364. In June 2015, while she triumphed as Joan of Arc in New York, Marion Cotillard made the news in Hollywood by registering her name in the cast of the next feature film by Robert Zemeckis, a spy thriller in which she should give the line to Brad Pitt.
365. *Ouest France*, November 25, 2013.
366. *Vogue Paris*, #929, August 2012.
367. Claire FORTIN, "A French actress in the heart of Hollywood," *Jour de France*, No. 48, March 2015.

me[368]." Let's not forget, she has come a long way, Marion having hated herself for years.

> "When I was very young, I wanted to be anyone but myself. I went through complicated periods where I totally rejected myself[369]."

Today she has managed to slip into the skin of herself and seems to be the happiest in the world.

"Her real success has been not to seek success[370]," wrote the polemist writer Yann Moix about her recently. Since *La Môme*, she has become the most *French of* stars across the Atlantic!

368. Dany Jucaud, "Marion Cotillard. La belle Américaine", *Paris Match*, n° 3170, 18 February 2010.
369. *Ibid*.
370. Yann Moix, "Marion Cotillard," *Paris Match*, no. 3430, February 12, 2015.

Epilogue

At 41 years old, Marion Cotillard has great projects coming up.

The most concrete: *Rock'n'Roll* and *Allies*.

Rock'n'Roll is the fifth film directed by Guillaume Canet. Several celebrities have joined the cast, such as Johnny Hallyday, Gilles Lellouche and Kev Adams[371]. It is an offbeat comedy whose *pitch*, which should have remained secret, was first revealed by the singer:

> "It's an idea from Guillaume Canet. Something really nice: a guy gets dumped by a girl who tells him: "You're not *rock and roll*!" To win her back, he absolutely wants to become *rock and roll* but loses it and does a lot of stupid things. And then one day, he decides to go see the boss of *rock and roll*, me. He asks me for advice and then everything goes to hell[372]."

371. See Mathilde DOIEZIE, "Guillaume Canet and Marion Cotillard, on-screen couple in *Rock'n'Roll*," *Le Figaro*, May 7, 2016 [online]. URL: <http://www.lefigaro.fr/cinema/2016/05/07/03002-20160507ARTFIG00055-guillaume-canet-et-marion-cotillard-en-couple-a-l-ecran-dans-rock-n-roll.php>. Accessed September 14, 2016.

372. lemonde.fr, October 2, 2015.

If Johnny Halliday is delighted with this confidence, the producer Alain Attal is less.

Shooting began on Monday, January 18, 2016 and spanned over nine weeks in Paris and in the studio. The release is expected to hit the screens in early 2017.

***

Allies is a film directed by Robert Zemeckis *(Forrest Gump*[373]*)*. As for him, it should be released on November 23, 2016 in the United States and land on French screens in the wake, Paramount Studios announced.

In this spy thriller set in the midst of World War II, a romance will develop between a French resistance fighter (Marion Cotillard) and an allied Canadian spy (Brad Pitt). The film was shot in part in London, where the reunion of the two actors accomplices made the happiness of the paparazzi in late March 2016.

In 2016, Marion Cotillard defended two feature films in competition at the 69th Cannes Film Festival, presided over by Australian George Miller (*Mad Max* saga).

---

373. American movie, with Tom Hanks, released in 1994.

The first, *Mal de pierres*, features Gabrielle, a young woman who has grown up in a small agricultural bourgeoisie in which her dream of absolute passion causes a scandal. An intimate, rural drama and, for *Télérama*, Nicole Garcia's best film.

Just the end of the world[374], the second one, is adapted from the eponymous play by Jean-Luc Lagarce. The story is that of a young author's afternoon with his family who, after twelve years of absence, returns to his native village to announce his impending death to his family. The subject is serious, hopeless. But for many, the Dolan magic works once again.

The love affair between Marion Cotillard and Cannes thus continues. Pregnant with her second child, she then set a year and a half of rest from October 2016, after finishing the shooting of Arnaud Desplechin's new film, *The Ghosts of Ishmael*.

She will, however, continue to promote her films, as she did in late 2016 for the release of *Assassin's Creed*, (expected on December 21).

Moments of happiness in perspective because Marion Cotillard, recently named Knight of the Legion of Honor, has been lucky enough to work with great directors who have offered her

---

374. Grand Prize and Ecumenical Jury Prize at the 2016 Cannes Film Festival.

magnificent roles. If the actress has the reputation of investing 1,000%, she is no less amazed by her exceptional career:

> "I am grateful to life and this journey to be able to meet such beautiful, inspiring and life-changing people[375]."

Marion Cotillard has the humility of the great.

375. *Version Femina*, No. 711, November 15, 2015.

FILMOGRAPHY

Cinema

— Feature films

Philippe HAREL, *L'Histoire du garçon qui voulait qu'on l'embrasse*, 1994, 95 minutes.

Arnaud DESPLECHIN, *Comment je me suis disputé... (ma vie sexuelle)*, 1996, 178 minutes.

Coline SERREAU, *La Belle Verte*, 1996, 99 minutes.

Gérard PIRÈS, *Taxi*, 1997, 90 minutes.

Francis REUSSER, *The War in the High Country*, 1999, 105 minutes.

Sarah LÉVY, *From Blue to America*, 1999, 100 minutes.

Gérard KRAWCZYK, *Taxi 2*, 2000, 88 minutes.

Alexandre AJA, *Furia*, 2000, 90 minutes.

Pierre GRIMBLAT, *Lisa*, 2001, 109 minutes.

Gilles PAQUET-BRENNER, *Les Jolies Choses*, 2001, 105 minutes.

Guillaume NICLOUX, *A Private Affair*, 2002, 107 minutes.

Gérard KRAWCZYK, *Taxi 3*, 2003, 87 minutes.

Yann SAMUELL, *Children's Games*, 2003, 93 minutes.

Tim BURTON, *Big Fish*, 2003, 125 minutes.

Jean-Pierre JEUNET, *Un long dimanche de fiançailles*, 2004, 134 minutes.

Tristan AUROUET and Gilles LELLOUCHE, *Narco*, 2004, 105 minutes.

Lucile HADZIHALILOVIC, *Innocence*, 2005, 120 minutes.

Steve SUISSA, *Cavalcade*, 2005, 90 minutes.

Rémi BEZANÇON, *Ma vie en l'air*, 2005, 103 minutes.

Richard BERRY, *The Black Box*, 2005, 87 minutes.

Stéphan GUÉRIN-TILLIÉ, *Edy*, 2005, 101 minutes.

Abel FERRARA, *Mary*, 2005, 85 minutes.

Fabienne GODET, *Sauf le respect que je vous dois*, 2006, 90 minutes.

Julie LOPES-CURVAL, *Toi et Moi*, 2006, 90 minutes.

Olivier VAN HOOFSTADT, *Dikkenek*, 2006, 85 minutes.

Lionel BAILLIU, *Fair Play*, 2006, 98 minutes.

Ridley SCOTT, *A Good Year* (2006), 2007, 118 minutes.

Olivier DAHAN, *La Môme*, 2007, 135 minutes.

Michael MANN, *Public Enemies*, 2009, 134 minutes.

Karim DIDRI, *The Last Flight*, 2009, 94 minutes.

Rob MARSHALL, *Nine*, 2010.

Christopher NOLAN, *Inception*, 2010, 148 minutes.

Guillaume CANET, *Les Petits Mouchoirs*, 2010, 154 minutes.

Woody ALLEN, *Midnight in Paris* (2011), 2011, 100 minutes.

Steven SODERBERGH, *Contagion*, 2011, 110 minutes.

Jacques AUDIARD, *Of Rust and Bone*, 2012, 122 minutes.

Christopher NOLAN, *The Dark Knight Rises*, 2012, 165 minutes.

Guillaume CANET, *Blood Ties*, 2013, 127 minutes.

James GRAY, *The Immigrant*, 2013, 120 minutes.

Adam McKay, *Anchorman 2: The Legend Continues*, 2013, 119 minutes.

Jean-Pierre and Luc DARDENNE, *Two Days, One Night*, 2014, 95 minutes.

Justin KURZEL, *Macbeth*, 2015, 113 minutes.

Xavier DOLAN, *Just the End of the World*, 2016, 95 minutes.

Nicole GARCIA, *Mal de pierres*, 2016, 120 minutes.

Robert ZEMECKIS, *Allies*, 2016.

Justin KURZEL, *Assassin's Creed*, 2016, 140 minutes.

Guillaume CANET, *Rock'n'Roll*, 2017.

Arnaud DEPLECHIN, *The Ghosts of Ishmael*, 2017.

— Short films

Olivier VAN HOOFSTADT, *Snuff Movie*, 1995, 13 minutes.

Mauro LOSA, *The Sentence*, 1996, 15 minutes.

Émmanuel HAMON, *Insalata Mista*, 1996, 6 minutes.

Olivier VAN HOOFSTADT, *Keo*, 1997, 11 minutes.

Luc GALLISSAIRES, *Classified Case*, 1998, 18 minutes. (Prize for best actress at the [1st] Rencontres cinématographiques d'Istres).

Mathieu MERCIER, *L'Appel de la cave*, 1999, 16 minutes.

Gilles PAQUET-BRENNER, *Le Marquis*, 2000.

Franck GUÉRIN, *Quelques jours de trop*, 2000, 31 minutes.

Céline NIESZAWER, *Heureuse*, 2001, 13 minutes.

Karim ADDA, *Boomer*, 2015, 15 minutes.

Television

— Series

Ray AUSTIN, *Saving Grace / An Immortal Passion* in *Highlander*, season 1, episode #17, 1992.

Dennis BERRY, *Nowhere to Run / State of Siege* in *Highlander*, season 1, episode #21, 1992.

Bernard DUBOIS, *Father and son* in *Extrême limite*, broadcast on TF1 on July 8, 1994.

Gilberto AZEVEDO, *La Pistonnée* in *Extrême limite*, broadcast on TF1 on August 24, 1994.

Yves AMOUREUX, *The news of the week* in *Théo, la tendresse*, broadcast on TF1 on January 5, 1996.

— Telefilms

Claude, *Le Monde des tout-petits* in the program *Les couleurs de la vie*, broadcast on TF1 on May 17, 1982.

Claude CAILLOUX, *Lucie*, in the program *D'hier et d'aujourd'hui*, broadcast on TF1 on January 24, 1983.

Dennis BERRY, *Chloé*, broadcast on France 2 on June 11, 1996.

Dominique TABUTEAU, *Interdit de vieillir*, broadcast on France 2 on June 3, 1998.

Nils TAVERNIER, "La Mouette" in *L'@mour est à réinventer*, broadcast on Arte on December 5, 1996, 5 minutes.

Valérie MÜLLER-PRELJOCAJ, *La Surface de réparation*, in the program *Libre court*, broadcast on France 3 on June 25, 1999.

Olivier MEGATON, *Doggy Dog*, in *Les Redoutables*, broadcast on 13e Rue on January 18, 2001.

Laurent CARCÉLÈS and Arnaud CÉLIGNAC, *Une femme piégée*, broadcast on M6 on February 21, 2001.

— Sketches

Renaud LE VAN KIM, *L'Ours*, in *Le Débarquement*, broadcast on Canal+ on January 18, 2013.

Ali MARHYAR and Pierre NINEY, *Battle the rap*, in *Casting(s)*, broadcast on Canal+ on May 13, 2015.

— Clips

LES WAMPAS, *Little girl*, 1990.

Tommy HOOLS, *Givin' Up*, 2003.

Hawksley WORKMAN, *No Reason to Cry Out Your Eyes*, 2004.

CALOGERO, Pascal OBISPO and Forent PAGNY, *Y'a pas un homme qui soit né pour ça*, "10 ans ensemble", 2004.

Beds are burning, Time for Climate Justice "Environmental Campaign", 2009.

YODELICE, *More Than Meets The Eyes & Breathe In*, 2010.

Franz FERDINAND, *Forehead Tittaes*, 2010.

David BOWIE, *The Next Day*, 2013.

— Advertisements

Gérard Jugnot, *Tu t'es vu quand t'as bu,* 1991.

Olivier Dahan, *The Lady Noire Affair*, 2009.

Jonas Akerlund, *Eyes of Mars by Lady Rouge*, 2010.

David Lynch, *Lady Blue Shanghai*, 2010.

John Mitchell Cameron, *Lady Grey London*, 2011.

John Mitchell Cameron, *L.A.dy Dior*, 2011.

Eliott Bliss and Marion Cotillard, *Lady Dior "Enter the Game,"* 2014.

Theater

Laurent Cotillard, *Y'a des nounours dans les placards*, at the Théâtre contemporain de la danse de Paris, 1997.

Opera

Paul Claudel and Arthur Honegger, *Joan of Arc at the stake*, 2005 (first performance) at the Palais des Sports in Orleans, 2005 then at the Auditorium in Barcelona, Spain, 2012 (broadcast on Medicis TV on November 17, 2012).

At the Rainier III Auditorium in Monte Carlo, Monaco; at the Halle aux Grains in Toulouse; at the Philharmonie de Paris; at Lincoln Center in New York - 2015].

Voxography

George MILLER, *Happy Feet*, 2006, 108 minutes. French voice of Gloria.

François and Jean-Jacques MANTELLO, *Voyage sous les mers 3D*, 2009, 81 minutes. Narrator.

Guillaume VINCENT, *Land of the Bears*, 2014, 87 minutes. Narrator.

Kyle BALDA and Pierre COFFIN, *The Minions*, 2015, 91 minutes.French voice of Scarlet Overkill.

Mark OSBORNE, *The Little Prince*, 2015, 106 minutes. Voice of the Rose.

Christian DESMARES and Franck EKINCI, *Avril et le monde truqué*, 2015, 103 minutes.Voice of Avril.

Shaun MONSON, *Unity*, 2015. Narrator.

Documentaries

Bastien DUVAL, *Mon clown*, broadcast on Canal+ on March 14, 2008.

Fabien CONSTANT, *Mademoiselle C.*, 2013, 93 minutes.

Frédéric TCHENG, *Dior and Me*, 2015, 86 minutes.

Documentation

In the press

Ciné-Télé-Revue, La Dépêche du Midi, Elle, L'Express Styles, Le Film Français, Le Figaro, Le Figaro Magazine, France Dimanche, Gala, Glamour, Grazia, Jour de France, Libération, Madame Figaro, Marie Claire, Nous Deux, Le Nouvel Observateur, Le Parisien, Paris Match, Le Point, Point de vue, Première, Psychologies Magazine, Question de femmes, Studio Magazine, Studio Ciné Live, Télé Poche, Télérama, Télé 7 jours, Télé-Star, Tv Magazine, Version Femina, Vogue Paris.

On line

www.wikipedia.org

www.ina.fr

www.ecranlarge.com

www.jpbox-office.com

www.imdb.com

www.allocine.fr

www.unifrance.org

FROM THE SAME AUTHOR

Biographies

- *CinéMarilyn ou l'Âge d'or des sex-symbols d'Hollywood et d'ailleurs*, éditions Publibook, Paris, 2006.
- *Brigitte Bardot : Le Mythe éternel*, collection "Temps mémoire", éditions Autres Temps, Marseille, 2009.
- *Martine Carol ou Le Destin de la Marilyn française*, preface by Brigitte Bardot, collection "Temps mémoire", éditions Autres Temps, Marseille, 2011.
- *Marilyn Monroe : d'hier à aujourd'hui*, preface by Brigitte Bardot, Mon petit éditeur, Paris, 2012.
- *Isabelle Adjani, la Magnifique*, Éditions Mustang, Chatou, 2014.

Novels

- *Even if...*, Éditions Bénévent, Nice, 2004.
- *Un pas dans le vide : roman gay*, Éditions gaies et lesbiennes, Paris, 2013.
- *The Gates of My House*, My Little Editor, Saint-Denis, 2016.

Theater

- *Muriel ou Le Temps d'aimer*, Mon petit éditeur, Paris.

Table of contents

Best sellers Max Milo Editions

Hitler's banker, Jean-François Bouchard

Confessions of a forger, Éric Piedoie Le Tiec

The Koran and the flesh, Ludovic-Mohamed Zahed

Governing by fake news, Jacques Baud

Governing by chaos, Collectif

A political history of food, Paul Ariès

Mad in U.S.A.: The ravages of the "American model",
Michel Desmurget

Mondial soccer club geopolitics, Kévin Veyssière

Putin: Game master?, Jacques Braud

Treatise on the three impostors: Moses, Jesus, Muhammad,
The Spirit of Spinoza

TV Lobotomy, Michel Desmurget